An Address to All Believers in Christ

By David Whitmer

Copyright © 2021 Lamp of Trismegistus. All rights reserved. No part of this publication may be reproduced or transmitted in any form or by any means, electronic or mechanical, including photocopying, recording, or by any information storage and retrieval system, without permission in writing from Lamp of Trismegistus. Reviewers may quote brief passages.

ISBN: 978-1-63118-545-8

*Mormon History
Series*

Other Books in this Series and Related Titles

Pearl of Great Price by Joseph Smith (978-1-63118-539-7)

The Angel of the Prairies or A Dream of the Future: Mormon History Series By Elder Parley Parker Pratt (978-1-63118-541-0)

A Manuscript on Far West by Reed Peck (978-1-63118-544-1)

The Story of Mormonism by James E Talmage (978-1-63118-543-4)

Interesting Account of Several Remarkable Visions: Mormon History Series By Orson Pratt (978-1-63118-553-3)

The Book of John Whitmer by John Whitmer (978-1-63118-554-0)

The Philosophy of Mormonism by James E Talmage (978-1-63118-542-7)

The Book of Abraham: Mormon History by George Reynolds (978-1-63118-540-3)

The Testament of Abraham by Abraham (978-1-63118-441-3)

Private Diary of Joseph Smith 1832-1834 (978-1-63118-546-5)

Times and Seasons Volume 1, Numbers 1-3 (978-1-63118-555-7)

Times and Seasons Volume 1, Numbers 4-6 (978-1-63118-556-4)

The Evening and Morning Star Volume 1, Numbers 1 & 2 (978-1-63118-547-2)

The Evening and Morning Star Volume 1, Numbers 3 & 4 (978-1-63118-548-9)

The Evening and Morning Star Volume 1, Numbers 5 & 6 (978-1-63118-549-6)

The Evening and Morning Star Volume 1, Numbers 7 & 8 (978-1-63118-550-2)

The Evening and Morning Star Volume 1, Numbers 9 & 10 (978-1-63118-551-9)

The Evening and Morning Star Volume 1, Numbers 11 & 12 (978-1-63118-552-6)

The Testament of Moses by Moses (978-1-63118-440-6)

The Book of the Watchers by Enoch (978-1-63118-416-1)

Audio Versions are also available on Audible, Amazon and Apple

Other Books in this Series and Related Titles

The Hidden Mysteries of Christianity by Annie Besant (978–1–63118–534–2)

Rosicrucian Rules, Secret Signs, Codes and Symbols by various (978-1-63118-488-8)

History and Teachings of the Rosicrucians by W W Westcott &c (978-1-63118-487-1)

Freemasonry and the Egyptian Mysteries by C. W. Leadbeater (978-1-63118-456-7)

The Book of Astronomical Secrets by Enoch (978-1-63118-443-7)

The Psalms of Solomon by King Solomon (978-1-63118-439-0)

The Historic, Mythic and Mystic Christ by Annie Besant (978–1–63118–533–5)

Masonic and Rosicrucian History by M P Hall & H Voorhis (978-1-63118-486-4)

American Indian Freemasonry by A C Parker (978-1-63118-460-4)

Some Deeper Aspects of Masonic Symbolism by A E Waite (978-1-63118-461-1)

Masonic Symbolism of King Solomon's Temple by A Mackey &c (978-1-63118-442-0)

The Old Past Master by Carl H Claudy (978-1-63118-464-2)

The Book of Parables by Enoch (978-1-63118-429-1)

The Secrets of Enoch by Enoch (978-1-63118-449-9)

Masonic Symbolism of the Apron & the Altar by various (978-1-63118-428-4)

The Book of Wisdom of Solomon by King Solomon (978-1-63118-502-1)

Masonic Symbolism of Easter and the Christ in Masonry (978-1-63118-434-5)

The Odes of Solomon by King Solomon (978-1-63118-503-8)

Ancient Mysteries and Secret Societies by M P Hall (978-1-63118-410-9)

The Golden Verses of Pythagoras: Five Translations (978-1-63118-479-6)

Book of Dreams by Enoch (978-1-63118-437-6)

A Few Masonic Sermons by A. C. Ward &c (978-1-63118-435-2)

Audio versions are also available on Audible, Amazon and Apple

Table of Contents

An Address to All Believers in Christ

Title Page...7

PART I

Chapter I...8
Chapter II...27

PART II

Chapter III...38
Chapter IV...45
Chapter V...65
Chapter VI...69
Chapter VII...76
Chapter VIII...80
Chapter IX...88
Chapter X...95
Chapter XI...100
Chapter XII...103

AN ADDRESS

TO

ALL BELIEVERS IN CHRIST.

BY

A WITNESS TO THE DIVINE AUTHENTICITY

OF THE BOOK OF MORMON.

DAVID WHITMER,

RICHMOND, MISSOURI.

1887

PART FIRST

CHAPTER I

Dear Reader:

Part first of this pamphlet is a brief address to those who have not read the Book of Mormon, and who are not conversant with the denominations that believe in that book.

Part second is an address to all believers in the Book of Mormon.

There are three distinct denominations that believe the Book of Mormon to be the Word of God:

First: *The Church of Christ.*

Second: *The Reorganized Church of Jesus Christ of Latter Day Saints.*

Third: *The Church of Jesus Christ of Latter Day Saints.*

The last named is the church in Salt Lake City; they believe in the doctrine of polygamy, while the two first named churches do not believe in that doctrine. I am an elder in "the Church of Christ." We believe in the doctrine of Christ as it is taught in the New Testament and the Book of Mormon, the same gospel being taught in both these books. The Bible being the sacred record of the Jews who inhabited the eastern continent; the Book of Mormon being the sacred record of the Nephites (descendants of Joseph, the son of Jacob), who inhabited the western continent, or this land of America. The Indians are the remnant of that people, who drifted into unbelief and darkness about 350 years after Christ appeared to them and established his church among them, after finishing his mission at Jerusalem. We believe in faith in Christ, repentance and baptism for the remission of sins, and the gift of the Holy Ghost. We believe in the laying on of hands as it was practiced in the days of the Apostles. We believe in the resurrection of the dead and eternal judgment. We also believe in the Words of Christ when he said, *"These signs shall follow them that believe."* Our belief concerning the order of offices in the church, etc., will be found in Part Second of this pamphlet. THE CHURCH OF CHRIST holds to the original doctrine and order that was first established upon the teachings of Christ in the written word, in 1829, when the Lord set his hand the second time to establish the true gospel upon the earth and recover his people, which is in fulfillment of the prophecies in the Bible. We denounce, the doctrine of polygamy and spiritual wifeism. It is a great evil, shocking to the moral sense, and the more so because practiced in the name of Religion. It is of man and not of God, and is especially forbidden in the Book of Mormon itself in these words. *"Behold, David and Solomon truly had many wives and concubines, which thing was abominable before me, saith the Lord.* * * * * * For there *shall not any man among you have save it be one wife: and concubines he shall have none: For I the Lord God, delighteth in the chastity of woman."* (Book of Mormon, page 116, chap. 2, par. 6). We do not indorse the teachings of any of the so-called Mormons or Latter Day Saints, which are in conflict with the gospel of our Lord and Saviour Jesus Christ, as taught in the New Testament and the Book of Mormon. They have departed in a great measure from the faith of the CHURCH OF CHRIST as it was first established, by heeding revelations given through Joseph Smith, who, after being called of God to translate his sacred word — the Book of Mormon — drifted into many errors and gave many revelations to introduce doctrines, ordinances and offices in the church, which are in conflict with Christ's teachings. They also changed the name of the church. Their departure from the faith is also according to prophecy. *"Now the spirit speaketh expressly that in THE LATTER TIMES some shall depart from the faith, giving heed to seducing spirits and doctrines of devils."* (1 Tim. iv : 1). On account of God giving to Joseph Smith the gift to translate the plates on which was engraven the Nephite scriptures, the people of the church put too much trust *in him* — in the *man* — and believed his words as if they were from God's own mouth. They have trusted in an arm of flesh. (Jeremiah xvii : 5) *"Thus saith the Lord : Cursed be the man that trusted in man, and maketh flesh his arm, and whose heart departeth from the Lord."* They looked to Joseph Smith as lawgiver; we look to *Christ alone*, and believe only in the religion of Jesus Christ and not in the religion of any man.

The doctrine of polygamy was not introduced until about fourteen years after the church was established; but other doctrines of error were introduced earlier than this. I left the body in June, 1838, being five years before polygamy was introduced.

Joseph Smith drifting into errors after translating the Book of Mormon, is a stumbling-block to many, but only those of very weak faith would stumble on this account. Greater abominations are recorded of

David in the Bible, than is recorded to-day of Joseph Smith; but do you reject the Psalms on this account? Do you reject the Proverbs because Solomon was a polygamist? Stop and think, you who are hasty to condemn. If you desire to know whether or not the Book of Mormon is true, read the book and investigate it, for Christ has promised that he who seeks in the right way shall find the truth of all things. We are commanded to *"Prove all things; hold fast that which is good."* (1 Thes. v : 21).

The Reorganized Church of Jesus Christ of Latter Day Saints, believe that Joseph Smith was a true prophet up to his death, and accept his revelations in their Book of Doctrine and Covenants. The revelation to practice polygamy is not printed in their Doctrine and Covenants. They do not believe in the doctrine of polygamy.

The Church of Jesus Christ of Latter Day Saints (the church at Salt Lake City) believe that Joseph Smith was a true prophet up to the time of his death, and accept his revelations which they have published in their Book of Doctrine and Covenants. In this book is the revelation on polygamy.

It is also a stumbling-block to those who desire to investigate as to the truth of the Book of Mormon, to see the believers in that book divided; but the divisions have been brought about by the revelations of Joseph Smith. We, the Church of Christ, who accept only the Bible and the Book of Mormon as the rule and guide to our faith , agree on the doctrine and gospel of Christ. The Book of Mormon comes forth claiming to be the scriptures of the tribe of Joseph, written by holy men of God, which record has been kept pure. It claims that when the Bible was written by the tribe of Judah (the Jews), it was plain to the understanding of men; and that many plain and precious things have been taken from it by a great and abominable church; and that on this account the Gentiles stumble over the true doctrine of Christ. The Book of Mormon comes forth claiming to make plain the doctrine of Christ as taught in the New Testament; and it a does make it so plain that a child can understand it. To all who are without prejudice, the Book of Mormon is the key to the understanding of the Bible. As I have stated, all who take it and the Bible alone as the guide to their faith, agree on the doctrine of Christ.

I know that reproach has been brought upon the Book of Mormon. Because some of those who believe it have drifted into wickedness, the world has rejected the book and turned it aside as a thing of naught; but if such persons will stop and think, they will see that they refuse to read this book, which claims to be a message from God, simply because some have transgressed who believe in the book! Such persons are not very earnestly seeking for truth. Those who have read the history of the apostolic church know, that before John wrote the Revelation, many of those who believed in Christ went into all manner of wickedness ad heresies, practicing those things in the name of Christ, and thereby brought reproach upon the name "Christian." Apostolic church history tells us that the Nicolaitanes (Rev. ii: 15), who departed from the faith by following Nicolas, one of the first seven deacons (Acts vi: 5)) were also called "Christians;" also that many factions which sprang out of the Christian church, also called themselves "Christians." The Nicolaitanes claimed that Nicolas had received a revelation from God to practice the doctrine of "free love," which is worse than polygamy. (Irenaeus, Epiphanius, Hippolytus.) Reproach was thus brought upon the name "Christian," just as it has been brought upon the words of Christ-the Book of Mormon. History tells us it was a disgrace in the eyes of the world to be called a "Christian," even during the days of the apostles. In Acts xxviii:22 we find that the true church was evil spoken *"For as concerning this sect, we know that everywhere it is spoken against."* Paul speaks of the reproach of Christ in Heb. xi:26 and xiii:13. Christ speaks of the reproach his disciples will have to bear for his name, telling them many times that his disciples would always be persecuted. Peter prophesied (2 Peter ii:1-2), that damnable heresies would be brought into the church; *"and many shall follow their pernicious ways, by reason of whom* THE WAY OP TRUTH *shall be evil spoken of."* So has it been in these last days. On account of the heresy of polygamy and other heresies, *"the way of truth"* is evil spoken of; and those who believe in *all* the scriptures of our Lord Jesus Christ, are called by the world "Mormons," and are looked upon with more or less shame by the majority of people; but we are willing to bear the reproach for Him who died for us, for *we know* that the Book of Mormon is His word, and by His word we can inherit eternal life if we are faithful in keeping His commandments. God's wisdom is not man's wisdom, and His ways are not man's ways. He works in a way least expected by man. He does his work in a way that all men may stumble and not understand, unless their whole heart and desire is upon God, and not upon the things of this world. *"Love not the world, neither the things, that are in the world. If any man love the world, the love of the Fother is not in him."* (1 John ii: 15.) *"Ye cannot serve God and mammon."* (Matt. vi: 24.) He who makes up his mind to serve God with an eye single to his glory, the light that is in him will not be darkness to the truth as it is in Christ; such a person will overcome the stumbling-blocks by the Holy Spirit enlightening his mind, and he will see and understand the truth. God works by stumbling-blocks. He ordained that Christ should come as a stumbling-block to the Jews, so that all who did not have an eye single to his glory might stumble and not understand. *"And He* (Christ) *shall be for a sanctuary; but for a stone of stumbling and for a rock of offense to both the houses of Israel, for a sin and for a snare to the inhabitants of Jerusalem. And many among them shall stumble, and fall, and be broken, and be snared, and be taken."* (Isaiah viii:14-15.) (See also 1 Peter ii:7-8, 1 Cor. i:23, Rom. ix: 32-33.) The Jews did not expect the Christ to come in the way he did, because the prophecies about his coming were obscure; so they rejected him.

The Gentiles cannot expect the words of Christ—the Book of Mormon—to come in the way it has, because the prophecies about its coming forth are obscure; so they have rejected it; but the stone which the builders have rejected, the same will become the head of the corner. The Book of Mormon is the word of God. The prophecies in the scriptures concerning the way in which Christ would come to the Jews, are obscure, but they are just as God wanted them. Likewise are the prophecies in the Bible concerning the coming forth of the word of Christ in these last days, which is *"the dispensation of the fullness of times."* The prophecies which foretell the coming forth of the Book of Mormon are fully as plain to the Gentiles, as the prophecies were to the Jews concerning Christ's coming. The people cannot understated why the Lord would bring forth his word from *"a book* (plates) *that is sealed"* and was buried in the ground by his ancient prophets on this land: and why He should have the words of the book delivered *"to one that is learned,"* telling him to read it, etc.; (see Isa. xxix) but the learned and wise men of the world could not read it; God gave to an unlearned boy, Joseph Smith, the gift to translate it by the means of a STONE. See the following passages concerning the *"Urim and Thummin,"* being the same means and one by which the Ancients received the word of the Lord. (1 Sam. xxviii:6. Neh. vii:65. Ezra ii:63. Num. xxvii:21. Deut. xxxiii:8. Exodus xxviii:30. Lev. viii:8.) But this is a great stumbling-block to the people now. They cannot understand why God would work in this manner to bring forth his word; and why he would choose such a man as Joseph Smith to translate it: and they think the canon of scripture is full: and that angels do not minister unto men in these days. But oh kind reader, if you desire to know the truth, be not hasty to condemn and judge, but I pray you to investigate. The scriptures teach that God works in a way least expected by men. *"Neither are your ways my ways, saith the Lord."* (Isa. LV:8). *How unsearchable are His judgments, and His ways past finding out."* (Rom. xi:33). Read Isa. xxix, whole chapter, which is a prophecy concerning the way in which the Book of Mormon was to come forth. *"Out of the ground;" " Out of the dust;"* From, *"the words of a Book* (plates) *that is sealed:"* The men of the world who are wise and prudent in the eyes of the world, shall be confounded; they will not understand the Lord's way of working. *"For the wisdom of their wise men shall perish, and the understanding of their prudent men shall be hid."* But the meek and lowly in heart will understand it. *"The meek also shall increase their joy in the Lord, and the poor among men shall rejoice in the Holy One of Israel."* And those who are spiritually blind and deaf shall *"hear the words of the Book,"* and *"see out of obscurity, and out of darkness." "They also that erred in spirit shall come to understanding, and they that murmured shall learn doctrine;"* (The above quotations are from the 29th chapter of Isaiah.) John, in his vision on the Isle of Patmos, of *"things which must be hereafter,"* saw *"Another angel fly in the midst of heaven, having the everlasting gospel to preach unto them that dwell ON THE EARTH."* (Rev. xiv:6.) In Isaiah xi:11—12, It is prophesied as follows : *"and it shall come to pass in that day* (dispensation) *that the Lord shall set his hand again the second time to recover the remnant of his people * * * * and he shall set up an ensign for the nations, and shall assemble the outcasts of Israel, ant1 I gather together the dispersed of Judah (the Jews) from the four corners of the earth."* The coming forth of the Book of Mormon is only a preparatory work for the great and "marvelous work" of God which is yet to come in gathering scattered Israel, which is spoken of so often through the prophets. The Book of Mormon contains many prophecies which are now and have been during my life, under course of fulfillment. It says that more records are yet to come forth from the *"book that is sealed,"* which book is the sacred scriptures or records of the people who inhabited this land of America.

The children of Israel are to be gathered by the record of Judah (the Bible); and the record of Joseph; of which record the Book of Mormon is only a part. I will now quote from Ezekiel xxxvii:16-21, which is plain concerning this matter. Remember that in ancient times, writing was engraved upon stone and upon metallic plates, and they also wrote upon parchment which they rolled around a stick. A roll of parchment was called a "stick."

"Moreover, thou son of man, take thee one stick, and write upon it, For Judah, and for the children of Israel his companions: then take another stick, and write upon it, For Joseph, the stick of Ephraim, and for all the house of Israel his companions: and join them one to another in one stick; and they shall become one in thine hand. And when the children of thy people shall speak unto thee, saying, Wilt thou not show us what thou meanest by these? say unto them, * * * * Thus saith the Lord God; Behold, I will take the children of Israel from among the heathen, whither they be gone, and will gather them on every side, and bring them into their own land."

It is evident that this, like many other prophecies, refers to the time when the Israel of God will be gathered together in righteousness and holiness; when the shall be God's holy people forever. It says in this chapter, 23d to 28th verses, that when they are gathered, they shall *"No more defile themselves with their idols * * * nor with any of their transgressions,"* and the Lord *"will cleanse them, so they shall be my people, and I will be their God."* * * * and *"they shall walk in my judgments * * * * * and (I) will set my sanctuary in the midst of them forevermore. * * * * And the heathen* (all who are not Israel) *shall know that I the Lord do sanctify Israel when my sanctuary shall be in the midst of them forevermore."* (Concerning a literal gathering of the House of Israel will be first some day, and the Gentiles last. It is through the *"fullness of the Gentiles,"* that the veil of blindness which is now over Israel, shall be taken away. The cup of iniquity of the Gentiles is almost full; then God will turn to Israel, for Israel is not cast away forever. *"Blindness in part is happened to Israel, until the fullness of the Gentiles be come in. * * * There shall come out of Sion, the Deliverer, and shall turn away ungodliness from Jacob."* (See Romans 11th chapter.)

It is recorded in the American Cyclopaedia and the Encyclopaedia Britannica, that I, David Whitmer, have denied my testimony as one of the three witnesses to the divinity of the Book of Mormon; and that the other two witnesses, Oliver Cowdery and Martin Harris, denied their testimony to that Book. I will say once more to all mankind, that I have never at any time denied that testimony or any part thereof. I also testify to the world, that neither Oliver Cowdery or Martin Harris ever at an time denied their testimony. They both died reaffirming the truth of the divine authenticity of the Book of Mormon. I was present at the death bed of Oliver Cowdery, and his last words were, *"Brother David, be true to your testimony to the Book of Mormon."* He died here in Richmond, Mo., on March 3d, 1850. Many witnesses yet live in Richmond, who will testify to the truth of these facts, as well as to the good character of Oliver Cowdery. The very powers of darkness have combined against the Book of

Mormon, to prove that it is not the word of God, and this should go to prove to men of spiritual understanding, that the Book is true. To show the reader what I have had to contend with, I give you below a copy of a leaflet which I had printed and distributed in March, 1881.

"A PROCLAMATION"

"Unto all Nations, Kindred Tongues and People, unto whom these presents shall come:

"It having been represented by one John Murphy, of Polo, Caldwell County, Mo., that I, in a conversation with him last summer, denied my testimony as one of the three witnesses to the 'BOOK OF MORMON.'

"To the end, therefore, that he may understand me now, if he did not then; and that the world may know the truth, I wish now, standing as it were, in the very sunset of life, and in the fear of God, once for all to make this public statement:

"That I have never at any time denied that testimony or any part thereof, which has so long since been published with that Book, as one of the three witnesses. Those who know me best, well know that I have always adhered to that testimony. And that no man may be misled or doubt my present views in regard to the same, I do a again affirm the truth of all of my statements, as then made and published.

" 'He that hath an ear to hear, let him hear;' it was no delusion! What is written is written, and he that readeth let him understand.

"And that no one may be deceived or misled by this statement, I wish here to state : that I do not indorse polygamy or spiritual wifeism. It is a great evil, shocking to the moral sense, and the more so, because practiced in the name of religion. It is of man and not of God, and is especially forbidden in the Book of Mormon itself.

"I do not indorse the change of the name of the church, for as the wife takes the name of her husband so should the Church of the Lamb of God, take the name of its head, even Christ himself. It is the Church of Christ.

"As to the High Priesthood, Jesus Christ himself is the last Great High Priest, this too after the order of Melchisedec, as I understand the Holy Scriptures.

"Finally, I do not indorse any of the teachings of the so-called Mormons, of Latter Day Saints, which are in conflict with the Gospel of our Lord and Savior Jesus Christ, us taught in the Bible and Book of Mormon; for the same gospel is plainly taught in both of these books as I understand the word of God.

"And if any man doubt should he not carefully and honestly read and understand the same, before presuming to sit in judgment and condemning the light, which shineth in darkness, and showeth the way of eternal life as out by the unerring hand of God.

"In the spirit of Christ who hath said: 'Follow thou me, for I am the life, the light and the way,' I submit this statement to the world. God in whom I trust being my judge as to the sincerity of my motives and the faith and hope that is in me of eternal life.

"My sincere desire is that the world may be benefited by this plain and simple statement of the truth.

"And all the honor be to the Father, the Son and the Holy Ghost, which is one God. Amen. DAVID WHITMER."

"RICHMOND, Mo., March 19, 1881."

" We, the undersigned citizens of Richmond, Ray County, Mo., where David Whitmer, has resided since the year A. D. 1838, certify that we have been long and intimately acquainted with him and know him to be a man of the highest integrity, and of undoubted truth and veracity.

"Given at Richmond, Mo., this March 19, A. D. 1881.

Gen. Alexander W. Doniphan.

Hon. Geo. W. Dunn, Judge of the Fifth Judicial Circuit.

Thos. D. Woodson, President of Ray Co. Savings Bank

J. T. Child, editor of *Conservator*.

H. C. Garner, Cashier of Ray Co. Savings Bank.

L. C. Cantwell, Postmaster, Richmond.

Geo. I. Wasson, Mayor

Jas. A. Davis, County Collector.

C. J. Hughes, Probate Judge and Presiding Justice of Ray County Court.

Geo. W. Trigg, County Clerk.

W. W. Mosby, M. D. W. A. Holman, County Treasurer.

J. S. Hughes, Banker, Richmond.

James Hughes, Banker, Richmond.

D. P. Whitmer, Attorney-at-Law.

Hon. Jas. W. Black, Attorney-at-Law.

Thos. McGinnis, ex-Sheriff Ray County.

J. P. Quesenberry, Merchant.

W. R. Holman, Furniture Merchant.

Lewis Slaughter, Recorder of Deeds.

Geo. W. Buchanan, M. D.

A. K. Reyburn."

From the Richmond, (Mo.) *Conservator*, March 24, 1881. AN EXPLANATION.

"Elsewhere we publish a letter from David Whitmer, an old and well-known citizen of Ray, as well as an indorsement of his standing as a man, signed by a number of the leading citizens of this community, in reply to some unwarranted aspersions made upon him.

"There is no doubt that Mr. Whitmer, who was one of the three witnesses of the authenticity of the gold plates, from which he asserts that Joseph Smith translated the Book of Mormon (a fac simile of the characters he now has in his possession with the original records), is firmly convinced of its divine origin, and while he makes no effort to obtrude his views or beliefs, he simply wants the world to know that so far as he is concerned there is no 'variableness or shadow of turning.' Having resided here for near a half of a century, it is with no little pride that he points to his past record with the conscionsness that he has done nothing derogatory to his character as a citizen and a believer in the son of Mary, to warrant such an attack on him, come from what source it may, and now with the lilies of seventy-five winters crowning him like an aureole, and his pilgrimage on earth well nigh ended, he reiterates his former statements, and will leave futurity to solve the problem that he was but a passing witness to its fulfillment. His attacks on the vileness that has sprung up with the Utah Church, must have a salutary effect upon those bigamists who have made adultery the corner-stone in the edifice of their belief."

Besides other false statements that are in the two encyclopaedias above mentioned is the old story of the Spaulding manuscript. That is, that one Solomon Spaulding who died in Amity, Penn., in 1816, had written a romance, the scene of which was among the ancient Indians who lived in this country. That Spaulding died before he published his romance, and that Sydney Rigdon got hold of the manuscript in a printing office and copied it; that subsequently the manuscript was returned to Solomon Spaulding; that thirteen years after the death of Spaulding, in 1829, Rigdon became associated with Joseph Smith, who read the Spaulding manuscript from behind a blanket to Oliver Cowdery, his amanuensis, who wrote it down. Hence the origin of the Book of Mormon. This is what is claimed by the enemies of the book: Satan had to concoct some plan to account for the origin of that book. I will say that all who desire to investigate the Spaulding manuscript story will not be obliged to go very far before they will see the entire falsity of that claim. I testify to the world that I am an eye-witness to the translation of the greater part of the Book of Mormon. Part of it was translated in my father's house in Fayette, Seneca County N. Y. Farther on I give a description of the manner in which the book was translated.

When the Spaulding story was made known to believers in the book, they called for the Spaulding manuscript, but it could not be found; but recently, thanks to the Lord, the original manuscript has been found and identified. It has been placed in the library of Oberlin college, Oberlin, Ohio, for public inspection. All who have doubts about it being the original Spaulding manuscript, can satisfy themselves by visiting Oberlin and examining the proofs. The manuscript is in the hands of those who are not believers in the Book of Mormon. They have kindly allowed the believers in the book to publish a copy of the manuscript, with the proofs that it is the manuscript of Solomon Spaulding. There is no similarity whatever between it and the Book of Mormon. Any one who investigates this question will see that the Spaulding manuscript story is a fabrication concocted by the enemies of the Book of Mormon, in order to account for the origin of that book. Neither Joseph Smith, Oliver Cowdery, Martin Harris or myself ever met Sydney Rigdon until after the Book of Mormon was in print. I know this of my own personal knowledge, being with Joseph Smith, in Seneca County , N. Y., in the winter of 1830, when Sydney Rigdon and Edward Partridge came from Kirtland, Ohio, to see Joseph Smith, and where Rigdon and Partridge saw Joseph Smith for the first time in their lives.

The Spaulding manuscript story is a myth; there being no direct testimony on record in regard to Rigdon's connection with the manuscript of Solomon Spaulding.

I have in my possession the original manuscript of the Book of Mormon, in the handwriting of Oliver Cowdery and others, also the original paper containing some of the characters transcribed from one of the golden plates, which paper Martin Harris took to Professor Anthon, of New York, for him to read *"the words of a book that is sealed:"* but the learned professor, although a great linguist could not read the language of the Nephites. There is some evidence in the American Cyclopaedia favorable to the Book of Mormon that I will speak of. It is as follows:

"Martin Harris called upon Prof. Anthon, of New York, with a transcript on paper which Smith had given him of the characters on one of the golden plates. 'This paper,' Prof. Anthon said, in a letter dated "New York, Feb. 17, 1834, 'was in fact a singular scroll. It consisted of all kinds of crooked characters, disposed in columns, and had evidently been prepared by some person who had before him at the time a book containing various alphabets. Greek and Hebrew letters, crosses and flourishes, Roman letters, inverted or placed sideways, were arranged and placed in perpendicular columns," etc. The *"learned"* could not read it, and the book was delivered to him that is not learned. I will quote two verses from the twenty-ninth chapter of Isaiah, which is the prophecy regarding this matter.

"And the vision all is become unto you as the words of a book that is sealed, which men deliver to one that is learned, saying, Read this, I pray thee: and he saith, I cannot, for it is sealed: and the book is delivered to him that is not learned, saying, Read this, I pray thee: and ha saith, I am not learned."

(Verses 11 and 12.) No man could read it, but God gave to an unlearned boy the gift to translate it.

I will now give you a description of the manner in which the Book of Mormon was translated. Joseph Smith would put the seer stone into a hat, and pout his face in the hat, drawing it closely around his face to exclude the light; and in the darkness the spiritual light would shine. A piece of something resembling parchment would appear, and on that appeared the writing. One character at a time would appear, and under it was the interpretation in English. Brother Joseph would read off the English to Oliver Cowdery, who was his principal scribe, and when it was written down and repeated to Brother Joseph to see if it was correct, then it would disappear, and another character with the interpretation would appear. Thus the Book of Mormon was translated by the gift and power of God, and not by any power of man.

The characters I speak of are the engravings on the golden plates from which the book was translated. They were engraved thereon by the hand of a holy prophet of God whose name was Mormon, who lived upon this land four hundred years after Christ. Mormon's son, Moroni, after witnessing the destruction of his brethren, the Nephites, who were a white race—they being destroyed by the Lamanites (Indians)—deposited the golden plates in the ground, according to a command of God. An angel of the Lord directed Brother Joseph to them. The language of the Nephites is called the reformed Egyptian language.

I will give you the preface to the Book of Mormon, written by Moroni, and translated in the same manner as the Book was translated.

PREFACE.
AN ACCOUNT WRITTEN BY THE HAND OF MORMON UPON PLATES TAKEN FROM THE PLATES OF NEPHI.

"Wherefore, it is an abridgement of the record of the people of Nephi, and also of the Lamanites; written to the Lamanites, who are a remnant of the house of Israel; and also to Jew and Gentile; written by way of commandment, and also by the Spirit of prophesy and of revelation. Written and sealed up, and hid up unto the Lord, that they might not be destroyed; to come forth by the gift and power of God unto the interpretation thereof; sealed by the hand of Moroni, and hid up unto the Lord, to come forth in due time by the way of Gentile; the interpretation thereof by the gift of God.

"An abridgement taken from the Book of Ether: also, which is a record of the people of Jared; who were scattered at the time the Lord confounded the language of the people, when they were building a tower to get to heaven: which is to show unto the remnant of the house of Israel what great things the Lord hath done for their fathers; and that they may know the covenants of the Lord, that they are not cast off forever; and also to the convincing of the Jew and Gentile that Jesus is the Christ, the Eternal God, manifesting himself unto all nations. And now if there are faults, they are the mistakes of men; wherefore, condemn not the things of God, that ye may be found spotless at the judgment seat of Christ." "MORONI."

ALSO THE TESTIMONY OF THE THREE WITNESSES.

"Be it known unto all nations, kindreds, tongues, and people, unto whom this work shall come, that we, through the grace of God the Father and our Lord Jesus Christ, have seen the plates which contain this record, which is a record of the people of Nephi, and also of the Lamanites, their brethren, and also of the people of Jared, who came from the tower of which hath been spoken; and we also know that they have been translated by the gift and power of God, for His voice hath declared it unto us; wherefore we know of a surety, that the work is true. And we also testify that we have seen the engravings which are upon the plates; and they have been shown unto us by the power of God, and not of man. And we declare with words of soberness, that an angel of God came down from heaven, and he brought and laid before our eyes, that we beheld and saw the plates, and the engravings thereon; and we know that it is by the grace of God the Father, and our Lord Jesus Christ, that we beheld and bear record that these things are true; and it is marvelous in our eyes, nevertheless, the voice of the Lord commanded us that we should bear record of it; wherefore, to be obedient unto the commandments of God, we bear testimony of these things. And we know that if we are faithful in Christ, we shall rid our garments of the blood of all men, and be found spotless before the judgment seat of Christ, and shall dwell with him eternally in the heavens. And the honor be to the Father, and to the Son, and to the Holy Ghost, which is one God. Amen.

OLIVER COWDERY,

DAVID WHITMER,

MARTIN HARRIS."

AND ALSO TESTIMONY OF EIGHT WITNESSES.

"Be it known unto all nations, kindreds, tongues, and people, unto whom this work shall come, that Joseph Smith, Jr., the translator of this work, has shown unto us the plates of which hath been spoken, which have the appearance of gold; and as many of the leaves as the said Smith hath translated, we did handle with our hands. and we also saw the engravings thereon, all of which has the appearance of ancient work, and curious workmanship. And this we bear record with words of soberness, that the said Smith has shown unto us, for we have seen and hefted, and known of a surety, that the said Smith has got the plates of which we have spoken. And we give our names unto the world to witness unto the world that which we have seen; and we lie not, God bearing witness of it.

CHRISTIAN WHITMER, HIRAM PAGE,

JACOB WHITMER, JOSEPH SMITH, SR.,

PETER WHITMER, JR., HYRUM SMITH,

JOHN WHITMER, SAMUEL H. SMITH."

Dear Reader:—I want to ask you this question, if you are an unbeliever in the Book of Mormon, and I hope you will study over it prayerfully. The testimony of seven men, Matthew, Mark, Luke, John, Paul, Peter and Jude, comes down to us eighteen hundred years old; you accept their testimony as true. To-day we have the testimony of eleven witnesses who have lived in our generation, one of which (myself) is still living—these eleven men having lived honorable and upright lives-but you reject their testimony and accept the testimony of the seven men who have been dead eighteen hundred years.

If you will not grant a possibility of the Book of Mormon being true, and sit in judgment and hastily condemn it after reading what I have written, you can surely see for yourself that your heart is full of prejudice, Remember that prejudice is not of God. It is the spirit that hastily condemned and stoned the prophets of God in all ages past. So beware, and look well to your own heart, that Satan does not blind your understanding to the truth. If you are open to investigation and conviction, I pray you to read the Book of Mormon with a prayerful heart. All persons who are spiritual, having a fair understanding of the scriptures, how they can read that Book and reject it, is very strange indeed. The Book carries conviction with it. The wise men of this world could never write a book like it. Any one without prejudice, who is honestly seeking for truth, can see the finger of God in that book. It makes plain the doctrines which are so obscure in the New Testament, and over which the religious world is divided. For instance, the mode of baptism; the "signs" or spiritual gifts which Christ said in plain words should follow them that believe in him. All who are not blinded to the understanding of the New Testament scriptures, will admit that the spiritual gifts should be with the believers in Christ to-day; that the reason why the spiritual gifts are not following the believers to-day, is because they have not that strong and living faith that the ancient church had—down to about 200 years after the death of the Apostles: the Book of Mormon explains this matter in full, Likewise many other questions of vital importance in the doctrine of Christ, which the Christian world has been contending and disputing about for ages, this Book comes forth from God to explain them.

As we know, Christ and the apostle have taught that man must worship God *in His appointed way;* that is, that they must be right as to the true points of Christ's doctrin: But because a man is right on the doctrine of Christ, having been rightly adopted into the Church of Christ, this alone will not entitle him to the highest glory hereafter. We are taught that we must endure faithful unto the end, and bring forth fruit. Coming into the fold of Christ is simply the birth into the church; we are then babes, and from a babe we must grow in charity, grace, and knowledge, on toward the full stature of the perfect man in Christ; and to grow, we must walk in the Spirit, having the fruits of the Spirit, which is *"love, joy, peace, long-suffering, gentleness, goodness, faith, meekness, temperance."* Then we are Christ's, and *"have crucified the flesh with the affections and lusts."* (Gal. v : 22-24). This is the subject that is nearest my heart. The Spirit of Christ in man. I could write volumes on this subject, but why should I, when God's Holy Word is so full upon this matter. Those who cannot understand from the Word of God regarding the boundless love and Spirit of Christ, which Spirit must be in man or he is not Christ's, they could not comprehend it from my writing, however eloquent I might be. It is a gift which God alone gives to man, when man complies with certain conditions of heart as laid down in God's Word. The object of this pamphlet is to guide some honest hearts into the true doctrine of Christ, hoping that when they have found the straight and narrow way, that they may continue to walk therein, and bring forth much fruit to the glory of God.

I desire to my a few words concerning the Holy Ghost, which is the Spirit of Christ—the greatest gift of God to man. Many people claim to have this gift. I am not judging anyone, but I will tell you how we can tell when we have the Spirit of Christ; and when we have not this feeling and spirit, we have not His Spirit. When we have the Spirit of Christ, our hearts are filled with the love of God that reaches out and takes in all men, even our enemies. We then have every particle of prejudice, malice, envy and hatred cast out of our hearts; we then have no hatred whatever toward any person, even an enemy. Remember the words of Christ: *"For if ye love them which love you, what reward have ye? Do not even the Publicans the same? But I say unto you, Love your enemies; bless them that curse you: do good to them that hate you. * * * That ye may be children of your Father which is in heaven."* Nothing short of this is the Spirit of Christ. By this you can know whether you have the Holy Ghost or not. This is the test.

The religion of Jesus Christ is embodied in one word, and that word is LOVE; it is the first and great commandment, for on it hangs the law and the prophets. Charity is the great lack of religious professors. As we love and judge others, so we will be judged at the last day. The principal idea in religion is the fatherhood of God, and brotherhood of man. Christ taught us to pray, *Our* Father who art in heaven. Our motive in serving God must be love and not fear. Those who have never had the gift of the Holy Ghost, cannot understand how a person could actually love and do good to any enemy; but those who have this gift can understand it and experience it. The natural man cannot understand some things of the Spirit of God, because they are spiritually discerned. (1 Cor. ii:14) He who cannot forgive an enemy and actually love him and do good to him, has not yet been born again, and has not the Spirit of Christ.

"Now if any man have ot the spirit of Christ, he is none of his." (Rom. viii:9) When a man has this spirit—which is the Holy Ghost—he loves all men so much that his greatest desire in this world is to do the greatest amount of good to his fellow-man that is possible. What is the greatest good I can do to my fellow-men? It is to turn their footsteps heavenward; to preach the gospel and the love of Christ to them. The spirit of Christ is unselfish. It will act in all men to-day as it did in Paul. He said: *"Not seeking mine own profit, but the profit of many, that they may be saved."* (1 Cor. x:33.) My soul enlarges when I contemplate this subject. My heart goes out in fervent zeal and love for the children of men, in my great desires for their salvation; but God is just, and in His wisdom we are here in this world to suffer trials for a season, which will work out for us a far more exceeding and eternal weight of glory, if we are faithful while here in this world. God has placed man on the earth to be a free agent unto himself, and he receives good or evil, truth or error, just according to the way his heart is inclined.

In chapter ii, I give a few quotations from the Book of Mormon. I would especially call the readers attention to chapter iv, in Part Second of this pamphlet, in which I explain how the church drifted in errors by giving heed to revelations that were given by Joseph Smith after he had translated the Book of Mormon.

I have briefly noticed some of the evidences of that Book, hoping that this pamphlet may fall into the hands of some honest hearts who love the Lord in deed and in truth; who are willing to take upon themselves reproach for the name of Christ, and that by reading this work they may be led to investigate the evidences of the truth of that Book—which are many—and become convinced that it is the Word of God. Part Second of this pamphlet is an address to the Latter Day Saints to point out the errors they are in. By reading the address to them you can understand the position of the CHURCH OF CHRIST, and how the Latter Day Saints have in a great measure departed from the faith of the church as it was first established. I will close this chapter by some quotations from the Book of Mormon, and a few remarks.

"And when ye shall receive these things (the Book of Mormon), I would exhort you that ye ask God, the eternal Father, in the name of

Christ, if these things are not true; and if ye shall ask with a sincere heart, with real intent, having faith in Christ, he will manifest the truth of it unto you, by the power of the Holy Ghost; and by the power of the Holy Ghost, ye may know the truth of all things." (Moroni x:l.)

"*For it* (the Book of Mormon) *shall be brought out of darkness unto light, according to the Word of God; yea, it shall be brought out of the earth, and it shall shine forth out of darkness, and come unto the knowledge of the people: and it shall be done by the power of God.* * * * * *It shall come in a day when the power of God shall be denied* (2 Tim. iii:5) *, and churches become defiled, and shall be lifted up in the pride of their hearts; yea, even in a day when leaders of churches, and teachers, in the pride of their hearts, even to the envying of them who belong to their churches; yea, it shall come in a day when there shall be heard of fires, and tempests, and vapors of smoke in foreign lands; and there shall also be heard of wars and rumors of wars, and earthquakes in divers places.*" (Book of Mormon, chap. iv, par. 2, 3.)

Dear reader, can you not discern the signs of the times? God is beginning to warn the inhabitants of the earth, and these signs shall increase. The fullness of the iniquity of the Gentiles is nigh at hand—in the Lord's manner of speaking. Christ says in the Book of Mormon, that destructions will come upon this nation if they do not repent. I cry unto you with all my soul, repent! repent! and seek unto God that you may know the truth of these things, whether that book is from God or not. It is truly the straight and narrow way. Straight means close, narrow, and difficult to find. Christ said, *"Straight is the gate, and narrow is the way, which leadeth unto life, and few there be that find it."* If the truth as it is in Christ is hid away down in the depths of the so-called Mormon Problem, it is truly the straight and difficult way to find. And I will say to all who desire to have part in the first resurrection, having the whole truth as it is in Christ, that in the depth of these seeming mysteries and stumbling- blocks, there you will find the Pearl of Great Price. May God help you dear reader, to break the bands of Satan—give up this vain world—and fulfill the mission for which the God of heaven created you into the world.

CHAPTER II

In this chapter I give a few quotations from the Book of Mormon. The words of Jesus Christ: "And I give you these commandments because of the disputations which have been among you. And blessed are ye if you have no disputations among you." "For thus it behooveth the Father that it (the Book of Mormon) should come forth from the Gentiles, that he may show forth his power unto the Gentiles, for this cause, that the Gentiles, if they will not harden their hearts, that they may repent and come unto me, and be baptized in my name, AND KNOW OF THE TRUE POINTS OF MY DOCTRINE." (Nephi viii:9 and ix:ll.) "Woe be unto him that crieth, All is well; yea, woe be unto him that hearkeneth unto the precepts of men, and denieth the power of God and the gift of the Holy Ghost."

(In 2 Tim. iii:1-5, Paul prophesied that *in the last days,* men shall have *a form of godliness, but deny the power thereof.* The *power* is the Holy Ghost, and its manifestations. Paul says in 1 Cor. xii:7, that "the manifestation of the Spirit is given to every man," that is, every man who has the Holy Spirit. To one is given one gift and to one another gift.) * * *

"Woe unto all those who tremble, and are angry because of the truth of God. For behold, he that is built upon the rock, receiveth it with gladness: and he that is built upon a sandy foundation, trembleth lest he fall. * * * But behold, there shall be many at that day, when I shall proceed to do a 'marvelous work' among them, that I may remember my covenants which I have made unto the children of men, that I may 'set my hand again the second time to recover my people,' (Isa. "& xi:ll) which are of the house of Israel; and also, that I may remember the promises which I have made unto thee, Nephi, and also unto thy father, that I would remember your seed; * * * many of the Gentiles shall say, A Bible, a Bible, we have got a Bible, and there cannot be any more Bible. But thus saith the Lord God: O fools, they shall have a Bible; and it shall proceed forth from the Jews, mine ancient covenant people. And what thank they the Jews for the Bible which they receive from them? Yea, what do the Gentiles mean? Do they remember the travels, and the labors, and the pains of the Jews, and their diligence unto me, in bringing forth salvation unto the Gentiles? O ye Gentiles, have ye remembered the Jews, mine ancient covenant people? Nay; but ye have cursed them, and have hated them, and have not sought to recover them. But behold, I will return all these things your own heads; for I, the Lord, hath not forgotten my people. Thou fool, that shall say, a Bible, we have got a Bible, and we need no more Bible. Have ye obtained a Bible, save it were by the Jews? Know ye not that there are more nations than one? Know ye not that I, the Lord your God, have created all men, and that I remember those who are upon the isles of the sea (Acts, xvii:26), and that I rule in the heavens above and in the earth beneath; and I bring forth my word unto the children of men, yea, even upon all the nations of the earth? Wherefore murmur ye, because that ye shall receive more of my word? *Know ye not that the testimony of two nations is a witness unto you that I am God, that I remember one nation like unto another?* Wherefore, I speak the same words unto one nation like unto another. And when the two nations shall run together, the testimony of the two nations shall run together also. And I do this that I may prove unto many, that I am the same yesterday, today, and forever; and that I speak forth my words according to mine own pleasure. And because that I have spoken one word, ye need not suppose that I cannot speak another; for my work is not yet finished; neither shall it be, until the end of man; neither from that time henceforth and forever. Wherefore, because that ye have a Bible, ye need not suppose that it contains all my words; neither need ye suppose that I have not caused more to be written: * * * For behold, I speak unto the Jews, and they shall write it; and I shall also speak unto the Nephites, and they shall write it; and I shall also speak unto the other tribes of the house of Israel, which I have led away (the ten lost tribes, supposed to be beyond the North Sea—from the Book of Esdras), and they shall write it; and I shall also speak unto all nations of the earth, and they shall write it. And it shall come to pass that the Jews shall have the words of the Nephites, and the Nephites shall have the words of the Jews: and the Nephites and Jews shall have the words of the lost tribes of Israel: and the lost tribes of Israel shall have the words of the Nephites and the Jews. And it shall come to pass that my people which are of the house of Israel, shall be gathered home unto the lands of their possessions; and my word shall also be gathered in one. And I will show unto them that fight against my word and against my people, who are of the house of Israel, that I am God, and that I covenanted with Abraham, that I would remember his seed forever. * * * For behold, except ye shall keep the commandments of God ye shall all likewise perish. * * * As many of the Gentiles as will repent, are the covenant people of the Lord; and as many of the Jews as will not repent, shall be cast off. * * * Woe unto them that turn aside the just for a thing of nought, and revile against that which is good, and say that it is of no worth (the Book of Mormon); for the day shall come that the Lord God will speedily visit the inhabitants of the earth; and in that day that they are fully ripe in iniquity, they shall perish. But behold, if the inhabitants of the earth shall repent of their wickedness and abominations they shall not be destroyed, saith the Lord of hosts." From the twelfth chapter of 2 Nephi:

"But he that believeth these things which I have spoken, him will I visit with the manifestations of my spirit, and he shall know and bear record." (Ether i:12.)

" But he that believeth these things which I have spoken, him will 1 "visit with the manifestationsl of my spirit, and he shall know and bear "record." (Ether i:1!Z.)

If any man will do his will, he SHALL KNOW of the doctrine, whether it be of God, or whether I speak of myself." (John vii:17)

I will say a word here in regard to a passage in Rev. xxii:18:

For I testify unto every man that heareth the words of the prophecy of this book (the Revelation of John), *if any man shall add unto these things, God shall add unto him the plagues that are written in this book."*

This means that no man shall add unto the prophecy of John's Revelation. It can be plainly seen that it does not refer to the Bible, because the books which compose our Bible were not compiled when the Revelation was written. All the other books which compose the Bible were afterward added to John's Revelation.

Our Bible comprises only the books which the canons decided to compile. There are many inspired books that have never come down to us. There are over fifteen books spoken of in the Bible that are not in the Bible. In. the following passages are some of the books spoken of that are not in the Bible. 2 Chron. ix:29. 1 Chron. xxix:29. Num. xxi:14. 1 Kings xi:41. 2 Chron. xiii:22. 2 Chron. xii:15. 2 Chron. xx:34. 2 Chron. xxvi:22. Gen. v:1. Ex. xxiv:7. 1 Sam. x:25. 1 Kings iv:32. 2 Chron. xii:15. In 1 Cor. v:9, a third epistle to the Corinthians is mentioned; we have only two. In Col. iv:16, the epistle from Laodicea. In Jude iii, a second epistle of Jude is spoken of; we have but one. I have a copy of the book of Jasher; It is spoken of in 2 Sam. i:18 and Joshua x:13.

I will give a few quotations from the Book of Mormon in regard to some points of doctrine over which the religious world is divided:

"Wherefore, I would exhort you, that ye deny not the power of God; for he worketh by power, according to the faith of the children of men, the same to-day and to-morrow, and forever. And again I exhort you, my brethren, that ye deny not the gifts of God, for they are many; and they come from the same God. And there are different ways that these gifts are administered; but it is the same God who worketh all in all; and they are given by the manifestation of the Spirit of God unto men, to profit them. For behold, to one is given by the Spirit of God, that he may teach the word of wisdom; and to another, that he may teach the word of knowledge by the same Spirit; and to another, exceeding great faith; and to another, the gifts of healing by the same Spirit. * * * (and so on, the different gifts which are enumerated by Paul in 1 Cor. xii.) * * * * and all these gifts of which I have spoken, which are spiritual, never will be done away, even so long as the world shall stand, only according to the unbelief of the children of men. Wherefore, there must be faith; and if there must be faith, there must also be hope; and if there must be hope, there must also be charity; and except ye have charity, ye can in no wise be saved in the kingdom of God." Moroni x:1.

"And he (Christ) said unto them, On this wise shall ye baptize; and there shall be no disputations among you. Verily I say unto you, that whoso repenteth of his sins through your words, and desireth to be baptized in my name, on this wise shall ye baptize them: Behold, ye shall go down and stand in the water, and in my name shall ye baptize them. And now behold, these are the words which you shall say, calling them by name, saying : Having authority given me of Jesus Christ, I baptize you in the name of the Father, and of the Son, and of the Holy Ghost. Amen. And then shall ye immerse them in the water, and come forth again out of the water." (Nephi v:8.)

"The manner which the disciples, who were called elders of the church, ordained priests and teachers. After they had prayed unto the Father in the name of Christ, they laid their hands upon them, and said, In the name of Jesus Christ I ordain you to be a priest; (or if he be a teacher), I ordain you to be a teacher, to preach repentance and remission of sins through Jesus Christ, by the endurance of faith on his name to the end. Amen. And after this manner did they ordain priests and teachers, according to the gifts and callings of God unto men; and they ordained them by the power of the Holy Ghost which was in them—*(Chapter 8, Book of Moroni.)*

"The manner of their elders and priests administering the flesh and blood of Christ unto the church. And they administered it according to the commandments of Christ; wherefore we know the manner to be true; and the elder or priest did minister it. And they did kneel down with the church, and pray to the Father in the name of Christ, saying, O God, the Eternal Father, we ask thee in the name of thy Son Jesus Christ, to bless and sanctify this bread to the souls of all those who partake of it, that they may eat in remembrance of the body of thy Son, and witness unto thee, O God, the Eternal Father, that they are willing to take upon them the name of thy Son, and always remember him, and keep his commandments which he hath given them, that they may always have his Spirit to be with them. Amen.—*(Chapter 4, Book of Moroni.)*

"The manner of administering the wine. Behold, they took the cup, and said, O God, the Eternal Father, we ask thee, in the name of thy "Son Jesus Christ, to bless and sanctify this wine to the souls of all those who drink of it, that they may do it in remembrance of the blood of thy Son which was shed for them, that they may witness unto thee, O God, the Eternal Father, that they do always remember him, that they may have his Spirit to be with them. Amen.—*(Chapter 5, Book of Moroni.)*

"And now I speak concerning baptism. Behold, elders, priests and teachers were baptized; and they were not baptized, save they brought forth fruit meet that they were worthy of it; neither did they receive any unto baptism, save they came forth with a broken heart and a contrite spirit, and witnessed unto the church that they truly repented of all their sins. And none were received unto baptism, save they took upon them the name of Christ, having a determination to serve him to the end. And after they had been received unto baptism, and were wrought upon and cleansed by the power of the Holy Ghost, they were numbered among the people of the Church of Christ, and their names were taken, that they might be remembered and nourished by the good word of God, to keep them in the right way, to keep them continually watchful unto prayer, relying alone upon the merits of Christ, who was the author and the finisher of their faith. And the church did meet together oft, to fast and to pray, and to speak one with another concerning the welfare of their souls: and they did meet together oft to partake of bread and wine, in remembrance of the Lord Jesus; and they were strict to observe that there should be no iniquity among them; and whoso was found to commit iniquity, and three witnesses of the church did condemn them before the elders; and if they repented not, and confessed not, their names were blotted out, and they were not numbered among the people of Christ; but as oft as they repented, and sought forgiveness, with real intent, they were forgiven. And their meetings were conducted by the church, after the manner of the workings of the Spirit, and by the power of the Holy Ghost; for as the power of the Holy Ghost led them whether to preach or exhort, or to pray or to supplicate, or to sing, even so it was done.—(*Chapter 6, Book of Mormon*).

Concerning a literal gathering of the Israel of God upon the earth in righteousness and holiness, see the passages of scripture which are given below.

The Book of Mormon contains prophesies concerning the gathering of Israel, which are much more full and explanatory. I will not go into detail on the teachings in the Book of Mormon in regard to this matter, trusting that all who have become interested in that Book will read it. Jer. xxxi.8-14. Israel shall be gathered, "and they shall not sorrow any more at all." Jer. xxxii:37-41. Israel shall be gathered, "and I will give them one heart, and one way, that they may fear me forever." Isa. liv:7, whole chapter, Isa. xi:ll-16, Ezek. xxxvii:15-28, Ezek. xxxiv:13-31.

Regarding the two foregoing passages, remember that this prophesy was given about 400 years after King David was dead. Ezek. xi:17-21. Rev. v:9-10. "And they sang a new song, saying, Thou art worthy, etc., * * * * "and hast made us unto our God kings and priests: and we "shall REIGN ON THE EARTH." At the end of the millenial reign on this earth; then comes the end of the world and the second and last resurrection. All of the dead shall then rise. Only the righteous shall rise at the first resurrection. (Rev. xx:4-8, and whole chapter.) At the end of the world is the final judgment, after which there shall be a new earth and a new heaven. Then a great voice out of heaven cried "Behold, the tabernacle of God is with men, and he will dwell with them, and they shall be his people, and God himself shall be with them, and be their God." (Rev. xxi:l-7.)

In regard to the gathering of a part of the house of Israel upon this land of America, which is the land God gave to the seed of Joseph (son of Jacob); and the gathering of a part of the house of Israel upon the land of Palestine, which is the land God gave to the Jews, I give you some of the words of Jesus Christ himself, which he spake to the people while he was upon this land, after finishing his mission at Jerusalem.

(Book of Mormon, Nephi ix:9-12 and x:l.)

"And it shall come to pass that I will establish my people, 0 house of Israel. And behold, this people will I establish in this land, unto the fulfilling of the covenant which I made with your father Jacob; and it shall be a new Jerusalem. And the powers of heaven shall be in the midst of this people; yea, even I will be in the midst of you. Behold, I am he of whom Moses spake, saying, A prophet shall the Lord our God raise up unto you of your brethren, like unto me, him shall ye hear in all things whatsoever he shall say unto you. And it shall come to pass that every soul who will not hear that prophet, shall be cut off from among the people. Verily, I say unto you, yea; and all the prophets from Samuel, and those that follow after, as many as have spoken, have testified of me. And behold ye are the children of the prophets; and ye are of the house of Israel; and ye are of the covenant which the Father made with your fathers, saying unto Abraham, And in thy seed, shall all the kindreds of the earth be blessed; the Father having raised me up unto you first, and sent me to bless you, in turning away every one of you from his iniquities; and this because ye are the children of the covenant. And after that ye were blessed, then fulfilleth the Father the covenant which he made with Abraham, saying, in thy seed shall all the kindreds of the earth be blessed, unto the pouring out of the Holy Ghost, through me upon the Gentiles, which blessing upon the Gentiles, shall make them mighty above all, unto the scattering of my people, O house of Israel: and they shall be a scourge unto the people of this land. Nevertheless, when they shall have received the fullness of my gospel, then if they shall harden their hearts against me, I will return their iniquities upon their own heads, saith the Father. And I will remember the covenant which I have made with my people, and I have covenanted with them, that I would gather them together in mine own due time; that I would give unto them again the land of their fathers, for their inheritance, which is the land of Jerusalem, which is the promised land unto them forever, saith the Father.

"And it shall come to pass that the time cometh, when the fullness of my gospel shall be preached unto them, and they shall believe in me, that I am Jesus Christ, the son of God, and shall pray unto the Father in my name. Then shall their watchmen lift up their voice; and with the voice together shall they sing; for they shall see eye to eye. Then will the Father gather them together again, and give unto them Jerusalem for the land of their inheritance. Then shall they break forth into joy—sing together ye waste places of Jersulem: * * * * * * "And then shall be brought to pass that which is written, Awake, awake again, and put on thy strength, O Zion; put on thy beautiful garments, O Jerusalem, the holy city, for henceforth there shall no more come into thee the uncircumcised and the unclean. Shake thyself from the dust; arise, sit down, O Jerusalem; loose thyself from the bands of thy neck, O captive daughter of Zion. For thus saith the Lord, Ye have sold yourselves for nought; and ye shall be redeemed without money. Verily, verily, I say unto you, that my people shall know my name; yea, in that day they shall know that I am he that doth speak.

"And then shall they say. How beautiful upon the mountains are the feet of him that bringeth good tidings unto them, that publisheth peace: that bringeth good tidings unto them of good, that publisheth salvation; that saith unto Zion, thy God reigneth! And then shall a cry go forth, Depart ye, depart ye, go ye out from thence, touch not that which is unclean; go ye out of the midst of her; be ye clean, that bear the vessels of the Lord. For ye shall not go out with haste, nor go by flight: for the Lord will go before you; and the God of Israel shall be your rearward. Behold, my servant shall deal prudently, he shall be exhalted and extolled, and be very high. As many were astonished at thee: (his visage was so marred more than any man, and his form more than the sons of men), so shall he sprinkle many nations; the kings shall shut their mouths at him, for that which had been told them shall they see; and that which they had not heard shall they consider. Verily, verily, I say unto you, all these things shall surely come, even as the Father hath commanded me. Then shall this covenant which the Father hath covenanted with his people, be fulfilled; and then shall Jerusalem be inhabited again with my people, and it shall be the land of their inheritance. And verily, I say unto you, I give unto you a sign, that ye may know the time when these things shall be about to take place, that I shall gather in from their long dispersion, my people, O house of Israel, and shall establish again among them my Zion. And behold, this is the thing which I will give unto you for a sign, for verily I say unto you, that when these things which I declare unto you, and which I shall declare unto you hereafter of myself, and by the power of the Holy Ghost, which shall be given unto you of the Father, shall be made known unto the Gentiles, that they may know concerning this people who are a remnant of the house of Jacob, and concerning this my people who shall be scattered by them (the Indians); * * * when these things come to pass, that thy seed shall begin to know these things, it shall be a sign unto them, that they may know that the work of the Father hath already commenced unto the fulfilling of the covenant which he hath made unto the people who are the house of Israel. And when that day shall come, it shall come to pass that kings shall shut their mouths; for that which had not been told them shall, they see; and that which they had not heard shall they consider. For in that day, for my sake shall the Father work a work, which shall be a great and a marvelous work among them; and there shall be among them those who will not believe it, although a man shall declare it unto them. But behold, the life of my servant shall be in my hand; therefore they shall not hurt him, although he shall be marred because of them. Yet I will heal him, for I will shew unto them that my wisdom is greater than the cunning of the devil. Therefore it shall come to pass, that whosoever will not believe in my words, who am Jesus Christ, whom the Father shall cause him to bring forth unto the Gentiles, and shall give unto him power that he shall bring them forth unto the Gentiles, (it shall be done even as Moses said,) they shall be cut off from among my people who are of the covenant; and my people who are a remnant of Jacob, shall be among the Gentiles, yea, in the midst of them, as a lion among the beasts of the forest, as a young lion among the flocks of sheep, who, if he go through, both treadeth down and teareth in pieces, and none can deliver. Their hand shall be lifted up upon their adversaries, and all their enemies shall be cut off. Yea, wo be unto the Gentiles, except they repent, for it shall come to pass in that day, saith the Father, that I will cut off thy horses out of the midst of thee, and I will destroy thy chariots, and I will cut off the cities of thy land, and throw down all thy strong holds; and I will cut off witchcrafts out of thy land, and thou shalt have no more soothsayers: thy graven images I will also cut off, and thy standing images out of the midst of thee; and thou shall no more worship the works of thy hands; and I will pluck up thy groves out of the midst of thee; so will I destroy thy cities. And it shall come to pass that all lyings, and deceivings, and envyings, and strifes, and priestcrafts and whoredoms, shall be done away. For it shall come to pass, saith the Father, that at that day, whosoever will not repent and come unto my beloved Son, them will I cut off from among my people, O house of Israel; and I will execute vengeance and fury upon them, even as upon the heathen, such as they have not heard.

But if they will repent, and hearken unto my words, and harden not their hearts, I will establish my church among them, and they shall come in unto the covenant, and be numbered among this the remnant of Jacob, unto whom I have given this land for their inheritance, and they shall assist my people, the remnant of Jacob; and also, as many of the house of Israel as shall come, that they may build a city, which shall be called the New Jerusalem; and then shall they assist my people that they may be gathered in, who are scattered upon all the face of the land, in unto the New Jerusalem. And then shall the power of heaven come down among them; and I also will be in the midst, and then shall the work of the Father commence, at that day even when this Gospel shall be preached among the remnant of this people. Verily, I say unto you, at that day shall the work of the Father commence among all the dispersed of my people; yea, even the tribes which have been lost, which the Father hath led away out of Jerusalem. Yea, the work shall commence among all the dispersed of my people, with the Father, to prepare the way whereby they may come unto me, that they may call on the Father in my name; yea, and then shall the work commence, with the Father, among all nations, in preparing the way whereby his people may be gathered home to the land of their inheritance. And they shall go out from all nations; and they shall not go out in haste, nor go by flight; for I will go before them, saith the Father, and I will be their rearward.

"And in the mouth of three witnesses shall these things be established; and the testimony of three, and this work, in the which shall be shown forth the power of God, and also His word, of which the Father, and the Son, and the Holy Ghost beareth record; and all this shall stand as a testimony against the world at the last day. And if it so be that they repent and come unto the Father in the name of Jesus, they shall be received into the kingdom of God. And now, if I have no authority for these things, judge, ye, for ye shall know that I have authority when ye shall see me, and we shall stand before God at the last day. Amen." (Ether ii).

"Hearken, O ye Gentiles, and hear the words of Jesus Christ, the Son of the living God, which he hath commanded me that I should speak concerning you, for behold, he commandeth me that I should write, saying: Turn, all ye Gentiles, from your wicked ways, and repent of your evil doings, of your lyings and deceivings, and of your whoredoms, and of your secret abominations, and your idolatries, and of your murders, and of your priestcrafts, and your envyings, and your strifes, and from all your wickedness and abominations, and come unto me, and be baptized in my name, that ye may receive a remission of your sins, and be filled with the

Holy Ghost, that ye may be numbered with my people, who are of the house of Israel." (Nephi chap. xiv.)

PART SECOND

CHAPTER III

TO BELIEVERS IN THE BOOK OF MORMON

Dear Brethren: The spirit of God moves upon me to send forth this epistle unto you. It is wisdom in God that these facts which I give you have not been made generally known long ago. But now the Spirit of God has made it manifest to me to make them known. The time is at hand to prepare for the day when the gospel will go to the house of Israel! It has been made known to me that when the gospel goes to the remnant of Jacob (the Lamanites), it must go to them as Christ has given it to us, the fullness of which is in the Book of Mormon and the New Testament. I know that the Latter Day Saints are teaching some errors in doctrine, and I hope to convince the honest in heart among them of this fact. The commands of God are strict, and his word is yea, yea, and nay, nay. It is a serious thing for man to add doctrines to the doctrine which Christ has taught in his word. Christ has taught that it is necessary to be abiding in his doctrine, and whosoever teaches more or less than the doctrine which he has taught in his word, is not of Him. He has taught but one doctrine. I do not mean to judge or condemn the Latter Day Saints. God is the judge. But I will speak the truth as the Spirit of God moves upon me to speak it, and I hope and pray that many will heed the truth—that they will lay aside all error, and come in upon the doctrine of Christ, as it is taught in the written word. I believe that the Latter Day Saints who are opposed to polygamy have done a great work and great good. I believe they have done a great work in carrying forth the Book of Mormon. We cannot always understand Gods ways of dealing with his people. God suffers men to be led into error because of their blindness of heart. He works with men only according to their faith and obedience; but now the Spirit of God is moving upon the Elders of the Church of Christ to go forth unto all the believers in the Book of Mormon, and unto all other people, crying repentance, and calling on them to heed to the teachings of Christ. I do not mean to persecute Joseph the translator of the Book of Mormon. I love him, and I love Joseph his son, and believe him to be a good man. Joseph, like many of those of old whom God had chosen, fell into error; and why should we want to follow any man into error? Should we put our trust in an arm of flesh? Nay, verily! There never lived but one perfect man, and that was Christ; and he is our only law-giver. Therefore we should take great heed and compare with the "written word" all doctrines, and laws and revelations coming through any man, for any man can fall into error and lead every one into error who trusts in man. God chooses the weak things of this world, so that man should not put their trust in man and make flesh their arm, but put their trust in God only. It is just, in God's wisdom, that every one who is not living sufficiently spiritual to discern between truth and error, *should be led into error.* God called Saul and many others of old who afterward fell into error and lost the Spirit, knowing that they would fall, so as to let every one be led into error by them who had such little faith in God as to make a man their God, and trust in "an arm of flesh," instead of putting their whole faith and trust in God only, and heeding Him only. God suffered them to be led into error because of their transgressions and lack of faith in Him. Christ ha8 spoken, and the voice of God has declared from the heavens : *"Hear ye him!"* His teachings in the Book of Mormon and the New Testament are the same.

But the Latter Day Saints have another book of doctrine—the "Doctrine and Covenants"—in which are doctrines that Christ never taught to the "twelve" at Jerusalem, nor to the "twelve" upon this continent. The Latter Day Saints believe these new doctrines, which do not agree with the teachings of Christ. Why do they believe them? Because they are putting too much trust in a man! This has been the mistake of God's people in all ages past. Read the scriptures and observe how very soon the great majority of God's people always fell into error by trusting in man. Men who were humble when God chose them, but afterward fell into error. If men do not live near enough to God to discern error when it comes—and it may appear as an angel of light—(for instance, polygamy)—God suffers them to be led into error because of their transgressions. See how many of the prophets whom God called afterward fell into error. Saul, David, Solomon, and many prophets in Israel.

Now, I do not judge, nor say whether Saul, David, Solomon, or Joseph will be saved or lost. These are all in the hands of a just God. Perhaps the errors of David were more grievous than those of Joseph. Now I hope you understand me. I am not persecuting Brother Joseph, and never did persecute him. Because he erred is no reason why I should not love him. God called him to translate his sacred word by the power and gift of God; but he was not called to set up and establish the church any more than any of us Elders were. This I will prove conclusively later on, from evidence which you are bound to accept.

The "CHOICE SEER," spoken of in the Book of Mormon is not Brother Joseph. I will give you here a brief outline concerning this "Choice Seer" who is yet to come forth. The *man who is not learned* (in 2 Nephi xi; 18), refers to Brother Joseph, but the "Choice Seer" (in 2 Nephi ii) is another man. He is to come from the Lamanites. He is to come from the fruit of the loins of Joseph (of Egypt), that seed being the *"branch which was to be broken off"* at Jerusalem, to whom this land was consecrated for their inheritance forever—being Lehi and his seed; Lehi's seed being little Joseph, who received this blessing from his father Lehi, that his seed should not be utterly destroyed; for *out of his seed* which should not all be destroyed (the Indians) should come to this "Choice Seer." This is the interpretation of this chapter. This "Choice Seer" will be of that seed. His name will be Joseph, and his father's name Joseph. He is to translate sealed records yet to come forth, (spoken of in 2 Nephi xi:18). *"And not to the bringing forth my word only, saith the Lord,* BUT TO THE CONVINCING THEM OF MY WORD." How many Indians did Brother Joseph convince? He never preached a sermon to them in his life to my knowledge. May God help you brethren to understand this chapter, for it can only be understood by the enlightening power of the Holy Ghost. It is very plain to me. I speak in full on this subject in chapter X.

I want to say to the Latter Day Saints, that the elders of the Church of Christ, in coming to them, come to them as their brethren, in love and in meekness. God forbid that we should persecute you, who have likewise taken upon yourselves the "shame of Christ" in this age of the world—which shame, in the eyes of the world, is believing the Book of Mormon. No; we love you, and by the help of God we will labor, trusting that the day is not far distant when the honest in heart among you, and among all believers in the Book of Mormon, and the world, may all be one with us upon the doctrine of Christ, working by the power and gifts of God to prepare the way for the gospel to go to the House of Israel. God only knows how I have grieved and suffered and plead with him for you for the past forty-eight years, that you might repent and be enlightened by the Holy Ghost to see the errors into which you have been led. To God belongs the mystery of his dealings with his people; he is allwise, and his ways are not man's ways. Mormon stood alone for many years, when the whole church of Nephites and Lamanites had every one gone into error and transgression. He stood alone, holding the authority, and prayed to God continually that he might go to them and preach to them; but the Lord forbid him to preach to them. Then let no man judge hastily as to my authority, lest he judge wrongly and continue in error; but go to God in prayer and fasting, and find out the truth, for the Holy Ghost will guide you into all truth. If you believe my testimony to the Book of Mormon; if you believe that God spake to us three witnesses by his own voice, then I tell you that in June, 1838, God spake to me again by his own voice from the heavens, and told me to "separate myself from among the Latter Day Saints, for as they sought to do unto me, so should it be done unto them." In the spring of 1838, the heads of the church and many of the members had gone deep into error and blindness. I had been striving with them for a long time to show them the errors into which they were drifting, and for my labors I received only persecutions. In June, 1838, at Far West, Mo., a secret organization was formed, Doctor Avard being put in as the leader of the band; a certain oath was to be administered to all the brethren to bind them to support the heads of the church in *everything they should teach*. All who refused to take this oath were considered dissenters from the church, and certain things were to be done concerning these dissenters, by Dr. Avard's secret band. I make no farther statements now; but suffice it to say that my persecutions, for trying to show them their errors, became of such a nature that I had to leave the Latter Day Saints; and, as I rode on horseback out of Far West, in June, 1838, the voice of God from heaven spake to me as I have stated above. I was called out to hold the authority which God gave to me.

I see from a letter written by the heads of the church, while they were in Liberty Jail, that they repented while in jail of having anything to do with this secret organization, and came out against Dr. Avard, declaring it all wickedness, and resolved to henceforth disapprobate everything that was not according to the gospel, and which was not of a bold, frank and upright nature. I quote from this letter, printed in the *Times and Seasons,* July, 1840:

"We farther caution our brethren against the impropriety of the organization of bands or companies, by covenants, oaths, penalties, or secrecies; but let the time past of our experience and suffering by the wickedness of Dr. Avard suffice. And let our covenants be that of the everlasting covenant, as it is contained in the Holy Writ, and the things which God has revealed unto us. Pre friendship always becomes weakened the very moment you undertake to make it stronger by penal oaths and secrecy. Your humble servants intend FROM HENCEFORTH to disapprobate everything that is not in accordance with the fullness of the gospel of Jesus Christ and which is not of a bold, frank and upright nature."

They were put in jail in November, after I had left them. Now you see why I left the Latter Day Saints. After I left them they say they gave me a trial and cut me off. About the same time that I came out, the Spirit of God moved upon quite a number of the brethren who came out, with their families. All of the eight witnesses who were then living (except the three Smiths) came out; Peter and Christian Whitmer were dead. Oliver Cowdery came out also. Martin Harris was then in Ohio. The church went deeper and deeper into wickedness. They were driven out of Missouri, and went to Nauvoo; and were driven out of Nauvoo, and went to Salt Lake, where they are to-day, believing in the doctrine of polygamy. Nearly all the members at Nauvoo went to Salt Lake. Only a very few rejected the revelation on polygamy. The Reorganization is built up principally of members—not of the old church—but new converts. The majority of those who did not go to Salt Lake are in the Reorganized Church to-day.

Many of the Reorganized Church have wondered why I have stood apart from them. Brethren, I will here tell you why. God commanded me by his own voice to stand apart from you. Many of you think that I have a desire to lead—to lead a church that believe as I do. I have no such desire. A one-man leader to the church is not the teachings of Christ. After Brother Joseph was killed, many came to me and importuned me to come out and be their leader; but I refused. With these statements, so you will understand me, I will proceed to show you how the heads of the church went into one error after another. I followed them into many errors in doctrine, which the Lord has since shown me, and which errors I have confessed and repented of, and will speak of in this pamphlet.

I am not preaching self-justification from being in errors in doctrine in the past. It is since 1847 that I have been shown all the errors into which had followed the heads of the church, and that when God's own due time came for building up the waste places of Zion, the Church of Christ must be established on the teachings of Christ, which teachings in their purity are in the new covenant of the Book of Mormon, and come forth to us to settle all disputations about doctrine, because many plain and precious things have been taken from the record of the Jews, and on all doctrinal points—order of church offices, etc.—we must rely upon it.

Christ commanded the Nephites to write his teachings, for they were to come down to us as the fullness of his gospel to us.

And why is it? Oh, why is it that you will not take the words of Christ himself, and lay down your contentions and disputations, taking his plain, simple teachings which he has given us in that book? As you know, the teachings of Christ are the same in the New Testament and in the Book of Mormon; but on account of the plain and precious things being taken from the Bible, there is room therein for disputations on some doctrinal points; but the teachings of Christ in the Book of Mormon are pure, plain, simple and full. Christ chose "twelve" and called them disciples or elders, not apostles, and the "twelve" ordained elders, priests and teachers. These are all the spiritual offices in the Church of Christ, and their duties are plainly given, The manner of baptism, and the manner of administering the flesh and blood of Christ, and everything pertaining to the Church of Christ is plainly set forth in the fullness of the gospel, as I will show you in this epistle.

Of course I do not mean to place one book ahead of the other. I am also called to bear witness that the Bible is true. The angel who declared unto us that the Book of Mormon was true, also declared unto us that the Bible was true. They are both the Word of God, and as it is prophesied, they both shall be one.

Concerning the question of my authority to administer in the ordinances of the Church of Christ, I have this to say: As I have stated, I was called out to hold the authority that God gave to me. I am not judging as to whose authority was good, or whose authority was not good. I am not judging as to any man's authority now to act in the church he is in. he has authority to act in the church he is in: but the Lord has made it known to me that no man has authority to act in "the Church of Christ," without being adopted therein according to the gospel of Christ.

I believe there are many honest hearts among all the orders of Latter bay Saints, and many in all churches, and in the world, that will yet come to a knowledge of the truth. Many of you believe, that because some of the spiritual gifts are with you, therefore you must be in the true doctrine of Christ; but this does not follow. The "signs" are produced in a believer by his faith. Some of the signs have been with all the factions who believe the Book of Mormon. If you have not charity, the signs will profit you nothing, Christ said, *Many will say to me in that day, Lord, Lord, have we not prophesied in thy name? and in thy name have cast out devils? And in thy name done many wonderful works? And then will I profess unto them, I never knew you."* (Matt. vii: 22-23.) No, brethren! do not think that because some of the spiritual gifts are with a church, that that church cannot be in error by teaching more or less than the doctrine of Christ.

CHAPTER IV

HOW THE CHURCH WAS ESTABLISHED IN THE BEGINNING, AND HOW THEY DRIFTED INTO ERROR.

In June 1829, the translation of the Book of Mormon was finished. God gave it to us as his Holy Word, and left us as men to work out our own salvation and set in order the Church of Christ according to the written word. He left us as men to receive of His Spirit as we walked worthy to receive it; and His Spirit guides men into all truth; but the spirit of man guides man into error. When God had given us the Book of Mormon, and a few revelations in 1829 by the same means that the Book was translated, commanding us to rely upon the written word in establishing the church, He did His part; and it left us to do our part and to be guided by the Holy Ghost as we walked worthy to receive. God works with men according to their faith and obedience. He has unchangeable spiritual laws which He cannot break; and He could not be so merciful as to give more of His Spirit to any man, than that man was worthy to receive by his faith and obedience.

In the beginning we walked humble and worthy to receive a great portion of the Spirit of God, and we were guided rightly at first in establishing the Church, but we soon began to drift into errors, because we heeded our own desires too much, instead of relying solely upon God and being led entirely by His Holy Spirit. How easy it is for a man to drift into errors, and think at the time that he is doing God's will. Brethren, few of us know how wily and cunning Satan works, and how easy a man can be deceived and led into errors. Satan works in many ways to lead the spiritual man into error step by step. I will state a few facts concerning some of Brother Joseph's errors in the beginning, also the errors of us all, in order to show you these most important truths, viz: How humble and contrite in heart a man must be to receive revelations from God: and how very weak man is, and how liable to be led into error, thinking at the time that he is doing God's will.

At times when Brother Joseph would attempt to translate, he would look into the hat in which the stone was placed, he found he was spiritually blind and could not translate. He told us that his mind dwelt too much on earthly things, and various causes would make him incapable of proceeding with the translation. When in this condition he would go out and pray, and when he became sufficiently humble before God, he could then proceed with the translation. Now we see how very strict the Lord is; and how he requires the heart of man to be just right in His sight, before he can receive revelation from him.

When the Book of Mormon was in the hands of the printer, more money was needed to finish the printing of it. We were waiting on Martin Harris who was doing his best to sell a part of his farm, in order to raise the necessary funds. After a time Hyrum Smith and others began to get impatient, thinking that Martin was too slow and under transgression for not selling his land at once, even if at a great sacrifice. Brother Hyrum thought they should not wait any longer on Martin Harris, and that the money should be raised in some other way. Brother Hyrum was vexed with Brother Martin, and thought they should get the money by some means outside of him, and not let him have anything to do with the publication of the Book, or receiving any of the profits thereof if any profits should accrue. He was wrong in thus judging Bro. Martin, because he was doing all he could toward selling his land. Brother Hyrum said it had been suggested to him that some of the brethren might go to Toronto, Canada, and sell the copy-right of the Book of Mormon for considerable money: and he persuaded Joseph to inquire of the Lord about it. Joseph concluded to do so. He had not yet given up the stone. Joseph looked into the hat in which he placed the stone, and received a revelation that some of the brethren should go to Toronto, Canada, and that they would sell the copy-right of the Book of Mormon. Hiram Page and Oliver Cowdery went to Toronto on this mission, but they failed entirely to sell the copy-right, returning without any money. Joseph was at my father's house when they returned. I was there also, and am an eye witness to these facts. Jacob Whitmer and John Whitmer were also present when Hiram Page and Oliver Cowdery returned from Canada. Well, we were all in great trouble; and we asked Joseph how it was that he had received a revelation from the Lord for some brethren to go to Toronto and sell the copy-right, and the brethren had utterly failed in their undertaking. Joseph did not know how it was, so he enquired of the Lord about it, and behold the following revelation came through the stone: *"Some revelations are of God: some revelations are of men: and some revelations are of the devil."* So we see that the revelation to go to Toronto and sell the copy-right was not of God, but was of the devil or of the heart of man. When a man enquires of the Lord concerning a matter, if he is deceived by his own carnal desires, and is in error, he will receive an answer according to his erring heart, but it will not be a revelation from the Lord. This was a lesson for our benefit and we should have profited by it in future more than we did. Without much explanation you can see the error of Hyrum Smith in thinking evil of Martin Harris without a cause, and desiring to leave him out in the publication of the Book; and also the error of Brother Joseph in listening to the persuasions of men and enquiring of the Lord to see if they might not go to Toronto to sell the copy-right of the Book of Mormon, when it was made known to Brother Joseph that the will of the Lord was to have Martin Harris raise the money.

Remember this matter brethren; it is very important. Farther on I will give you references of scripture on this point, showing that this is God's way of dealing with His people. Now is it wisdom to put your trust in Joseph Smith, and believe all his revelations in the Doctrine and Covenants to be of God? Every one who does not desire to be of Paul, or of Apollos, or of Joseph, but desires to be *of Christ* will say that it is not wisdom to put our trust in him and believe his revelations as if from God's own mouth! I will say here, that I could tell you other false revelations that came through Brother Joseph as mouthpiece, (not through the stone) but this will suffice. Many of Brother Joseph's revelations were never printed. The revelation to go to Canada was written down on paper, but was never printed. When Brother Joseph was humble he had the Spirit of God with him; but when he was not humble he did not have the Spirit. Brother Joseph gave many true prophesies when he was humble before God: but this is no more than many of the other brethren did. Brother Joseph's true prophesies were almost all published, but those of the other brethren were not. I could give you the names of many who gave great prophesies which came to pass. I will name a few: Brothers Ziba Peterson, Hiram Page, Oliver Cowdery, Parley P. Pratt, Orson Pratt, Peter Whitmer, Christian Whitmer, John Whitmer, myself and others had the gift of prophesy. Hiram Page prophesied a few days before the stars fell in November, 1833, that the stars would fall from heaven and frighten many people. This prophesy was given in my presence. I could give you many instances of true prophesies which came through the above named brethren, but I desire to be brief. I could also tell you of some false prophesies which some of them gave, when they were not living humble.

After the translation of the Book of Mormon was finished, early in the spring of 1830, before April 6th, Joseph gave the stone to Oliver Cowdery and told me as well as the rest that he was through with it, and he did not use the stone any more. He said he was through the work that

God had given him the gift to perform, except to preach the gospel. He told us that we would all have to depend on the Holy Ghost hereafter to be guided into truth and obtain the will of the Lord. The revelations after this came through Joseph as "mouth piece;" that is, he would enquire of the Lord, pray and ask concerning a matter, and speak out the revelation, which he thought to be a revelation from the Lord; but sometimes he was mistaken about it being the word of the Lord. As we have seen, some revelations are of God and some are not. In this manner, through Brother Joseph as "mouth piece" came every revelation to establish new doctrines and offices which disagree with the New Covenant in the Book of Mormon and New Testament! I would have you to remember this fact.

In June, 1829, the Lord called Oliver Cowdery, Martin Harris, and myself as the three witnesses, to behold the vision of the Angel, as recorded in the fore part of the Book of Mormon, and to bear testimony to the world that the Book of Mormon is true. I was not called to bear testimony to the mission of Brother Joseph Smith any farther than his work of translating the Book of Mormon, as you can see by reading the testimony of us three witnesses.

In this month I was baptized, confirmed, and ordained an Elder in the Church of Christ by Bro. Joseph Smith. Previous to this, Joseph Smith and Oliver Cowdery had baptized, confirmed and ordained each other to the office of an Elder in the Church of Christ. I was the third person baptized into the church. In August, 1829, we began to preach the gospel of Christ. The following six Elders had then been ordained: Joseph Smith, Oliver Cowdery, Peter Whitmer, Samuel H. Smith, Hyrum Smith, and myself. The Book of Mormon was still in the hands of the printer, but my brother, Christian Whitmer, had copied from the manuscript the teachings and doctrine of Christ, being the things which we were commanded to preach. We preached, baptized and confirmed members into the Church of Christ, from August, 1829, until April 6th, 1830, being eight months in which time we had proceeded rightly; the offices in the church being Elders, Priests and Teachers. Now, when April 6, 1830, had come, we had then established three branches of the "Church of Christ," in which three branches were about seventy members: One branch was at Fayette, N.Y.; one at Manchester, N.Y., and one at Colesville, Pa. It is all a mistake about the church being *organized* on April 6, 1830, as I will show. We were as fully *organized*—spiritually—before April 6th as we were on that day. The reason why we met on that day was this; the world had been telling us that we were not a regularly organized church, and we had no right to officiate in the ordinance of marriage, hold church property, etc., and that we should organize according to the laws of the land. On this account we met at my father's house in Fayette, N.Y., on April 6, 1830, to attend to this matter of organizing according to the laws of the land; you can see this from Sec. 17 Doctrine and Covenants: the church was organized on April 6th *"agreeable to the laws of our country."*

It says after this, *"by the will and commandments of God;"* but this revelation came through Bro. Joseph as "mouthpiece." Now brethren, how can it be that the church was any more organized—spiritually—on April 6th, than it was before that time? There were six elders and about seventy members before April 6th, and the same number of elders and members after that day. We attended to our business of organizing, according to the laws of the land, the church acknowledging us six elders as their ministers; besides, a few who had recently been baptized and not confirmed were confirmed on that day; some blessings were pronounced, and we partook of the Lord's supper.

I do not consider that the church was any more organized or established in the eyes of God on that day than it was previous to that day. I consider that on that day the first error was introduced into the Church of Christ, and that error was Brother Joseph being ordained as "Prophet Seer and Revelator" to the church.

The Holy Ghost was with us in more power during the eight months previous to April 6, 1830, than ever at any time thereafter. Almost everyone who was baptized received the Holy Ghost in power, some prophesying, some speaking in tongues, the heavens were opened to some, and all the signs which Christ promised should follow the believers were with us abundantly. We were an humble happy people, and loved each other as brethren should love.

Just before April 6, 1830, some of the brethren began to think that the church should have a leader, just like the children of Israel wanting a king. Brother Joseph finally inquired of the Lord about it. He must have had a desire himself to be their leader, which desire in any form is not of God, for Christ said *"If any man desire to be first, the same shall be last of all, and servant of all." "He that would be great, let him be your servant." "For he that is least among you all, the same shall be great."* A true and humble follower of Christ will never have any desire to lead or be first, or to seek the praise of men or brethren. Desiring any prominence whatever is not humility, but it is pride; it is seeking praise of mortals instead of the praise of God. Joseph received a revelation that he should be the leader; that he should be ordained by Oliver Cowdery as "Prophet Seer and Revelator" to the church, and that the church should receive his words as if from God's own mouth. Satan surely rejoiced on that day, for he then saw that in time he could overthrow them. Remember, *"Some revelations are of God; some revelations are of man, and some revelations are of the devil."* God allowed them to be answered according to their erring desires. They were like the children of Israel wanting a king, and God gave them a king, but it was to their final destruction. He gave the church a leader, but it proved their destruction and final landing of the majority of them in the Salt Lake valley in polygamy, believing that their leader had received a revelation from God to practice this abomination. This was the first error that crept into the church. None of us detected it then. We had all confidence in Brother Joseph, thinking that as God had given him so great a gift as to translate the Book of Mormon, that everything he would do must be right. That is what I thought about it. You see how we trusted too much in man instead of going to God in humility, and to his written word, to see if we were proceeding rightly. It grieves me much to think that I was not more careful, and did not rely upon the teachings of Christ in the written word. But we were then young in years, and all of us were mere babes in Christ. Brother Joseph and myself were only twenty-five years of age.

Although Brother Joseph was in this high office, he was humble most of the time, and he and all of us had the Spirit with us when we were humble, but as I have stated we did not have the Spirit with us in power as a body after this, as we did before April 6, 1830. After Sydney Rigdon came into the church—or in the spring of 1831—we began to make proselytes faster; but great numbers coming into the church does not always signify great *spiritual* prosperity. The people made light of the church in Noah's time, there was only eight members in it, but it proved to be the true church.

I want the brethren to understand me concerning this error of ordaining Brother Joseph to that office on April 6, 1830. Not at all do I mean to say that I believe the church was then rejected of God. What occur[r]ed on that day was this: One of the elders of the church (Joseph) was led into a grievous error; and the members acquiesced in it. In time it proved to be a most grievous error, being the cause of the trouble which afterwards befel[l] the people of God. They put their trust in Brother Joseph and received his revelations as if from God's own mouth. (Jer.

xvii:5) *"Thus saith the Lord: cursed be the man that trusteth in man, and maketh flesh his arm; and whose heart departeth from the Lord."* This has been the great curse of the work of God in these last days. Nearly all of the church have continued to heed the words of men as if from God's own mouth—following man into one error in doctrine after another—from year to year—even on down into the doctrine of polygamy.

When Christ came into the world, the doctrine of a one man leader to the church *was not taught by Him, and we are positively under Christ and his teachings in the written word.* The Book of Morman [Mormon] tells us plainly that THE WORDS OF CHRIST ARE TO BE MADE KNOWN IN THE SEALED RECORDS OF THE NEPHITES, AND IN THE RECORD OF THE JEWS: (the Bible) and this excludes the Book of Doctrine and Covenants. (1 Nephi iii:43). (Concerning a "Choice Seer," who is to bring forth more of the words of Christ from the sealed records of the Nephites, and convince and restore the Lamanites and the house of Israel, See chapter 10). The next grievous error which crept into the church was in ordaining high priests in June, 1831. This error was introduced at the instigation of Sydney Rigdon. The office of high priests was never spoken of, and never thought of being established in the church until Rigdon came in. Remember that we had been preaching from August, 1829, until June, 1831—almost two years—and had baptized about 2,000 members into the Church of Christ, and had not one high priest. During 1829, several times we were told by Brother Joseph that an elder was the highest office in the church. In December, 1830, Sydney Rigdon and Edward Partridge came from Kirtland, Ohio, to Fayette, N.Y., to see Brother Joseph, and in the latter part of the winter they returned to Kirtland. In February, 1831, Brother Joseph came to Kirtland where Rigdon was. Rigdon was a thorough Bible scholar, a man of fine education, and a powerful orator. He soon worked himself deep into Brother Joseph's affections, and had more influence over him than any other man living. He was Brother Joseph's private counsellor, and his most intimate friend and brother for some time after they met. Brother Joseph rejoiced, believing that the Lord had sent to him this great and mighty man Sydney Rigdon, to help him in the work. Poor Brother Joseph! He was mistaken about this, and likewise all of the brethren were mistaken; for we thought at that time just as Brother Joseph did about it. But alas! in a few years we found out different. Sydney Rigdon was the cause of almost all the errors which were introduced while he was in the church. I believe Rigdon to have been the instigator of the secret organization known as the "Danites" which was formed in Far West Missouri in June, 1838. In Kirtland, Ohio, in 1831, Rigdon would expound the Old Testament scriptures of the Bible and Book of Mormon (in his way) to Joseph, concerning the priesthood, high priests, etc., and would persuade Brother Joseph to inquire of the Lord about this doctrine and that doctrine, and of course a revelation would always come just as they desired it. Rigdon finally persuaded Brother Joseph to believe that the high priests which had such great power in ancient times, should be in the Church of Christ to-day. He had Brother Joseph inquire of the Lord about it, and they received an answer according to their erring desires. Remember that this revelation came like the one to ordain Brother Joseph "Prophet Seer and Revelator" to the church—through Brother Joseph as mouthpiece, and not through the stone. Remember also that *"some revelations are of God; some revelations are of man; and some revelations are of the devil."*

False spirits, which come as an Angel of Light, are abroad in the earth to deceive, if it were possible, the very elect. Those whom Satan can deceive and lead into error he deceives. Now do not understand me to say that I think a man who is deceived about high priests being in the church is going to lose his soul. I am not judging—God is the judge. But if God did not mean for this order of high priests to be ordained in the Church of Christ, it is a serious error to have added that office to the Church. If God did not mean for Brother Joseph to set himself up as Seer to the church, and the church to receive his revelations as if from God's own mouth, I tell you brethren it is a most serious error. If you are in error on the gathering of Israel and building the city New Jerusalem, (and you are in error), it is a serious error; and likewise the other doctrines of error which are taught in the Book of Doctrines and Covenants.

In this manner the revelations came through Brother Joseph as mouthpiece from time to time. Brother Joseph would listen to the persuasions of men, and inquire of the Lord concerning the different things, and the revelations would come just as they desired and thought in their hearts.

In another part of this pamphlet I devote a chapter to the subject of High Priests. I will remark here, that in that chapter I give you the solemn news—at least, news to many of you—that when the first high priests were ordained at Kirtland, Ohio, in June 1831, the devil caught and bound two of the high priests as soon as they were ordained. Harvey Whitlock, who the devil caught, bound and twisted his face into demon-like shape, also John Murdock, who the devil bound so he could not speak. Thus showing that God's displeasure was upon their works when they ordained the first high priests in the church. None of the brethren understood this fact then. We still thought that anything Brother Joseph and Sidney Rigdon would do, must be all right and according to the will and mind of the Lord. The whole church acquies[c]ed in the error of ordaining high priests. Marvel not that we began to be led in to error so soon; the children of Israel went into gross error in forty days, following Aaron while Moses was in the mount.

I desire to say a few words here concerning prophets falling into error. Solomon, David, Saul, Uzziah and many great and gifted prophets in Israel fell into gross error, and some of them into crime. Paul said he kept his body under subjection, lest he should become a castaway, after having preached to others. Many of the Latter Day Saints believe that it is impossible for Brother Joseph to have fallen. I will give you some evidence upon this matter which I suppose you will certainly accept, showing that Brother Joseph belonged to the class of men who could fall into error and blindness. From the following you will see that Brother Joseph belonged to the weakest class—the class that were very liable to fall. I quote from a revelation which came through the stone, July, 1828. It is a revelation to Brother Joseph, chastising him for his errors after he had commenced to translate the Book of Mormon, telling him how often he had erred and transgressed the commandmants and the laws of God; telling him that if he was not aware, he would fall, and have his gift to translate taken from him. Also telling him, that although a man may have many revelations, and have power to do many mighty works, yet, if he boasts in his own strength, etc., he must fall. *"Remember, remember, that it is not the work of God that is frustrated, but the work of men: for although a man may have many revelations, and have power to do many mighty works, yet, if he boasts in his own strength, and sets at naught the counsels of God, and follows after the dictates of his own will and carnal desires, HE MUST FALL and incur the vengeance of a just God upon him. Behold, you have been entrusted with these things, but how strict were your commandments; and remember, also, the promises which were made to you, if you did not transgress them, and behold, HOW OFT HAVE YOU TRANSGRESSED THE COMMANDMENTS AND THE LAWS OF GOD, and have GONE ON IN THE PERSUASIONS OF MEN * * * Behold thou art Joseph, and thou wast chosen to do the wor[k] of the Lord,* (was given a gift to translate the Book) *but because of transgression, IF THOU ARE*

*NOT AWARE, THOU WILT FALL, but remember God is merciful: * * * * * thou hast suffered the council of thy Director to be trampled upon from the beginning."* So we see that Brother Joseph was very weak and liable to fall, even while translating the Book, the time when he should have been strong, because he was in constant communion with God. Now if he was so weak and liable to err *at that time,* is it any wonder that he erred in 1830, and after that time? Of course not! Ah brethren, great are the mysteries of God! His ways are not man's ways. He chooses the weak things of earth—weak men—so that man should not put his trust in man and make flesh his arm, but put his trust in God only, and rely upon that which is written. God put man on the earth to be a free agent unto himself, to choose and discern between good and evil, between truth and error in doctrine. It is necessary for man to be tempted and tried in every way conceivable, in order for him to prove himself, and overcome every snare, device, and stumbling-block of satan, to fit him for a higher state of happiness hereafter. You know the Scriptures teach that Satan's devices may appear as an Angel of Light; for instance, a false doctrine being revealed to a prophet who gives it to a church as if it came from God. When the devices of Satan do appear in this way, every man who is not living sufficiently humble to have a good portion of God's Spirit to detect the error, is led into believing it: and it is justice in God's wisdom that he should be thus led, because of his not living as he should live so as to have more of the Holy Ghost.

Now you have thought that because Brother Joseph was given a gift to translate the Book, that he could not fall into error; and you worship and give credit to *the man,* when all the credit is due to God. You should think of this matter. Brother Joseph did not write a word of the Book of Mormon; it was already written by holy men of God who dwelt upon this land. God gave to Brother Joseph the gift to see the sentences in English, when he looked into the hat in which was placed the stone. Oliver Cowdery had the same gift at one time. Now when we look at it aright, the fact of Brother Joseph having the gift to translate the Book, is that any reason why you should put any more trust in him than any other man? Not at all. Is that any reason why he should be a man who could not fall? Not at all. As you see from what the Lord told him, he was very weak man, and liable to fall even while translating the Book. *"How oft have you transgressed the commandments and the laws of God, and have gone on in the persuasions of men. * * * If thou art not aware thou wilt fall. * * * Thou hast suffered the counsel of thy Director to be trampled upon from the beginning. * * * Thou wilt* *again be called to the work; and except thou do this (repent) thou shalt be delivered up and become as other men, and have no more gift."* (To translate.) I give you my testimony that the Lord had to chastise Brother Joseph time and again, as a father would a disobedient child, to help him through the translation of the Book. God knows that I do not mean to persecute Brother Joseph. As I have said, I loved him. I am not crying him down or preaching self-righteousness, but I desire to get you to comprehend the sin of trusting in an arm of flesh, by receiving Brother Joseph's revelations as if they were from God's own mouth, when some of his revelations conflict with the teachings of Christ in the two sacred books. I tell you brethren, you are trusting in an arm of flesh and being in blindness you cannot see it.

I will now pass over a recital of the errors which came into the church by revelation from time to time, and speak of them hereafter. I desire to speak here on the subject of polygamy. A few years ago I had doubts in regard to Brother Joseph's connection with the Spiritual Wife doctrine, but I have recently seen Vol. I, No. 1, of the old Latter Day Saints *Herald,* which has settled this matter in my mind. The great majority of the Reorganized Church do not believe that Brother Joseph received the revelation on polygamy. I will say to them, that on their account it is with reluctance that I speak upon this subject; but on account of the honest in heart who have not yet read and believed the Book of Mormon, it is not with reluctance that I speak of it. I believe that this matter of polygamy is to-day the great stumbling-block to many who would accept the Book of Mormon, but they cannot understand how the Book could be true, if Joseph Smith received that revelation on polygamy. The fact cannot be denied that the world (with very few exceptions outside of the Reorganized Church) believes firmly that Brother Joseph received that revelation, or that he taught and practiced polygamy near the close of his life in Nauvoo. Now, on account of honest enquirers as to the truth of the Book of Mormon, it is necessary that I speak upon this matter. I am constantly receiving letters of inquiry as to my belief and knowledge concerning the question of polygamy. I have also another important reason for speaking upon this subject: There are false doctrines of importance in the book of Doctrine and Covenants, and I desire to prove them false doctrines, and get you to lay them aside and believe only what Christ taught and meant for us to believe. This was Christ's mission into the world. It is the mission of all the servants of God; to root out all false doctrine and error. So do not think that I mean to persecute you, or that I am striving for the mastery.

If Brother Joseph received the revelation on polygamy and gave it to the church, the book of Doctrine and Covenants must be laid down, because the commandment is, "His word ye shall receive as if from mine (God's) own mouth." Then you must receive the revelation on polygamy, or else you must lay aside the Doctrine and Covenants:

For his word (all of his word) ye *shall* receive as if from God's own mouth.

I now have as much evidence to believe that Brother Joseph received the revelation on polygamy and gave it to the church, as I have to believe that such a man as George Washington ever lived. I never saw General Washington, but from reliable testimony I believe that he did live.

I have the evidence regarding this revelation, that is recorded in Vol. 1, No. 1, *Latter Day Saints' Herald;* being evidence from your own side, which you are bound to accept. It is the evidence of some of the leaders of the Reorganization in the beginning, some of whom were with Brother Joseph in Nauvoo up to the time of his death. These articles appeared in the first number that was ever printed of the *Saint's Herald.* This number of the *Herald* is very scarce now: they seem to have been hid away and destroyed. I see that when the Reorganized Church was established, the fact that Joseph received this revelation was then known and acknowledged in editorials in the *Herald.* The reason why these articles were written in the *Herald,* was to explain why the Reorganized Church rejected the revelation received by Brother Joseph on polygamy, and to explain that he repented of his connection with polygamy just previous to this death.

As time rolled on, many of the Reorganization saw that to continue to acknowledge that Brother Joseph received this revelation, would bring bitter persecution upon themselves, as the public feeling at that time was very bitter. Will God approve of a church being built up upon representations of the innocence of Joseph Smith regarding polygamy, if he is not innocent in matter? Nay, verily! And I tell you that the efforts of the Reorganized Church in this regard have not been acceptable to God! He does not want any truth covered up. The inspired writers did not try to hide the polygamy of David and Solomon. Their transgressions do not make the Psalms and Proverbs untrue, neither do the errors of Joseph make the Book of Mormon untrue. God does not want any one in the church whose faith is so weak that he stumbles because of the transgressions *of any man or men*. Our faith and trust must be *in God*, and not in *any man!* It is the secret of your trouble. All of you believe the revelations of Joseph Smith as if they were from the mouth of God. You should have acknowledged belief in the errors of Joseph Smith, and not tried to hide them when there is so much evidence that he did go into error and blindness; you should have explained by the scriptures how that many of the prophets of old did the same thing, but that does not make the Book of Mormon untrue. There is abundant scripture to make his question very clear to any one. The leaders of the Reorganized Church, after a time, began to suppress their opinions concerning this matter. They would answer the question when asked about it, *"I do not know whether Joseph Smith received that revelation or not."* This was a truthful but evasive answer, as it was not a matter of knowledge, except with a few. All, or nearly all, of the pioneers of the Reorganization who were living in Nauvoo in 1843 and 1844 have now passed away, and you see what time has done in this regard. To-day nearly all of the Reorganization do not believe that Brother Joseph received that revelation on polygamy, or ever had any connection whatever with the doctrine of polygamy, openly and firmly denying this fact; some through ignorance, and some who should not be so ignorant about this matter. They charge it all to Brigham Young. Now, all honest men will understand, after they have read this pamphlet through, that I am doing God's will in bringing the truth to light concerning the errors of Brother Joseph. They will see that it is necessary, as he is the man who introduced many doctrines of error into the Church of Christ; and his errors must be made manifest and the truth brought to light, in order that all Latter Day Saints shall cease to put their trust in this man, believing his doctrines as if they were from the mouth of God.

I quote from Volume 1, Number 1, of *The True Latter Day Saints Herald,* page 24, from an article written by Isaac Sheen, who was a leader in establishing the Reorganization. "The Salt Lake apostles also excuse themselves by saying that Joseph Smith taught the spiritual wife doctrine, but this excuse is as weak as their excuse concerning the ancient kings and patriarchs. *Joseph Smith repented of his connection with this doctrine, and said that it was of the devil. He caused the revelation on that subject to be burned,* and when he voluntarily came to Nauvoo and resigned himself into the arms of his enemies, *he said that he was going to Carthage to die.* At that time he also said that, *if it had not been for that accursed spiritual wife doctrine, he would not have come to that.* By his conduct at that time he proved the sincerity of his repentance, and of his profession as a prophet. *If Abraham and Jacob by repentance can obtain salvation and exaltation, so can Joseph Smith."* Here we have Isaac Sheen's testimony as follows: That Joseph Smith did have connection with this spiritual wife doctrine; that he repented of it just before his death, having come to the conclusion that the revelation was not of God, but was of the devil; and he caused the revelation to be burned. Brother Sheen does not state how long Brother Joseph had connection with this doctrine, but of course we suppose from the time the revelation was given, July 12, 1843, until the time of his repentance just before his death, in June, 1844; at which time he concluded that the revelation was not of God, but was of the devil, and caused it to be burned, voluntarily giving himself up to his enemies, saying he was going to Carthage to die.

I will now quote from the same number of the *Herald,* page 8. It is an editorial, being the second article in the first number of the paper.

"This adulterous spirit (polygamy) had captivated their hearts and they desired a license from God to lead away captive the fair daughters of His people, *and in this state of mind they came to the Prophet Joseph* (not Brigham Young). Could the Lord do anything more or less than what Ezekiel hath prophesied (answer a prophet according to his iniquity). The Lord hath declared by Ezekiel what kind of an answer he would give them, therefore he answered them according to the multitude of their idols; (giving them an answer through Joseph—the revelation on polygamy; and Joseph gave the revelation to them—the church). Paul had also prophesied that for this cause 'God shall send them strong delusion, that they shall believe a lie; that they all might be damned who believed not the truth, but had pleasure in unrighteousness.' Both these prophecies agree. In Ezekiel's prophecy the Lord also says, 'I will set my face against that man, and will make him a sign and a proverb, and I will cut him off from the midst of my people; and ye shall know that I am the Lord. And if the prophet be deceived when he hath spoken a thing, I the Lord have deceived that prophet (or, allowed the prophet to be deceived because of his iniquity—W), and I will stretch out my hand upon him and will destroy him from the midst of my people Israel. And they shall bear the punishment of their iniquity; the punishment of the prophet shall be even as the punishment of him that seeketh unto him; that the house of Israel may go no more astray from me, neither be polluted any more with all their transgressions; but that they may be my people, and I may be their God, saith the Lord God.' We have here the facts as they have transpired, and as they will continue to transpire in relation to this subject. The death of the prophet is one fact that has been realized; *although he abhorred and repented of this iniquity before his death."*

Here we have also the testimony of the editor of the *Herald.*

On page 22, in the same number of the *Herald,* is an article of like testimony, by Wm. Marks, who, as he states in his article, was Presiding Elder at Nauvoo in 1844, when Brother Joseph was killed, and was with Brother Joseph up to his death. His testimony is the same as that given in the two foregoing articles.

He states that Brother Joseph said to him *just before his death,* concerning polygamy as follows: "He (Joseph) said it eventually would prove the overthrow of the church, and we should soon be obliged to leave the United States unless it could be speedily put down. He was satisfied that it was a cursed doctrine, and that there must be every exertion made to put it down, etc."

The reader will please notice this fact in regard to Wm. Marks' statement; and that is *the time* when Brother Joseph told him that polygamy must be put down in the church. *The time* when Brother Joseph said this to Wm. Marks, was just before his (Joseph's) death. Polygamy had then been in the church almost a year, and it was just before his death that Brother Joseph saw that polygamy was a cursed doctrine, and repented of his connection with that doctrine—believing then that the revelation was not of God, but was of the devil—and he then caused the revelation to be burned.

The foregoing evidence is sufficient to convince any one that Brother Joseph received the revelation on polygamy; that he gave the doctrine to the church; that he had connection with this spiritual wife doctrine himself; and afterwards became convinced that this revelation was of the devil, and repented of this iniquity just before his death.

Now brethren of the Reorganization, you must accept this revelation on polygamy, or else you must lay aside the book of Doctrine and Covenants; for the commandment is, His word ye shall receive as if from God's own mouth. Words would not come from God to practice polygamy, and after his people had practiced it for some time, then the word come that the revelation was of the Devil, and to repent of it. So we see that the commandment to receive Brother Joseph's words as if from

God's own mouth was false. Now, this commandment is in the revelation given April 6, 1830, the revelation for Brother Joseph to be ordained Seer to the Church. Now, can you not see that this revelation for Brother Joseph to be ordained Seer to the Church was false? Of course it was. There is no doubt about it. "Some revelations are of God; some revelations are of man; and some revelations are of the Devil." This is what God gave us through the stone in 1829 as I have before stated, for a warning to us all. The revelation given through Brother Joseph as mouthpiece on April 6, 1830, that he should be ordained Seer to the Church, after God had commanded him that He would grant him no other gift but to translate the Book of Mormon, I give you my testimony brethren that this revelation is not of God.

Now, how can you place full confidence in the revelations in the book of Doctrine and Covenants?

Why, oh! why is it that you will continue to trust in an arm of flesh? Why will you cling to Joseph Smith, who was only a man, and believe all his revelations as if they were from God's own mouth? Joseph Smith cannot save you in eternity! Cease to trust in him or in any other man; turn away from man entirely, and do not consider any man, but look to God and to his written word, for BY IT shall you be judged at the last day, and *not* by the book of Doctrine and Covenants.

If Christ did not mean for Brother Joseph to be ordained a Seer to the church, it is a most serious error. If Christ did not mean for three first presidents to be ordained in his church, it is a most serious error to have ordained them. If Christ did not mean for high priests to be ordained in his church, it is a most serious error to have ordained them. If Christ did not mean for the doctrine of "baptism for the dead" to be an ordinance in his church, it is a serious error. If you are in error concerning the "gathering" and building the city New Jerusalem, it is a serious error. If Christ did not mean for them to change the name which he gave the church in 1829, it is a serious error; and likewise other errors taught in the book of Doctrine and Covenants; as the doctrine of revenge—cursing one's enemies in the name of the Lord; etc. For the Salt Lake church, I will also add, the doctrine of polygamy and other doctrines which are not to be found in the teachings of Christ. So you see that if you are in error in taking the book of Doctrine and Covenants as the law of God to the church, you are in many grave and serious errors. The object of this epistle is to show you that you are in serious error in taking that book as a law of

God to the church; and that God's law is all contained in the written word—the Bible and the Book of Mormon.

Concerning the matter, if Joseph Smith received the revelation on polygamy, how can the Book of Mormon be true? I must say that all who stumble because of the errors of Joseph Smith, are weak indeed. It is on this account, and on account of the transgressions of some who have believed the Book of Mormon, that the world will not read and investigate as to the truth of that book, which claims to be the word of God to this generation. All those who reject it on this account should also reject the Psalms and Proverbs, because of David and Solomon's connection with polygamy. In the first place, the revelation on polygamy did not come by the same means as did the Book of Mormon. The Book of Mormon was translated from golden plates by the gift and power of God, by means prepared of God—the stone of which I have spoken. Soon after Brother Joseph finished the translation, he gave up the stone, and all his revelations after that—including the one on polygamy—he gave by his own mouth. The revelation on polygamy was given fourteen years after the translation of the Book of Mormon, and after Brother Joseph had drifted into error and blindness. As I have stated, the scriptures are plain concerning the matter of a prophet or any man once chosen of God, being afterwards deceived and led into error.

When a prophet, or any other man, prays to God and asks wisdom concerning a matter, his conscience will reveal an answer to him just according to the desires of his heart. If his desires are in any way carnal, he being deceived, an answer will be revealed to him accordingly; and he will think it is the revealed will of God. Satan reveals his will to a man, mixed with much truth and scripture in order to deceive him, and makes it appear as an Angel of Light. (2 Corinthians xi:14.,) *And no marvel; for Satan himself is transformed into an Angel of Light."* This is a mystery to a great many people, but only to those who are weak and have need of milk that they may grow in spiritual knowledge to understand the word of God. It is Satan who deceives the man, but God permits it because of the wicked desires of the man, and it is right and justice in God's wisdom to permit the persistent transgressor to be led off and deceived by a delusive false doctrine. Paul, in 2 Thess. ii:11, says: "And for this cause God shall send them strong delusion, that they should believe a lie." Why would God do this? Verses 10 and 12 give the reason why; "because they received not the love of the truth." * * * because they "believed not the truth, but had pleasure in unrighteousness." In Isaiah lxvi:2-4, the Lord says: "But to this man will I look, even to him that is poor and of a contrite spirit, and trembleth at my word." But to the people who "have chosen their own ways, and their soul delighteth in their abominations (polygamy), I will also choose their delusions." In Ezekiel xiv:4-9 we read: "Thus saith the Lord God; every man of the house of Israel that setteth up his idols in his heart, and putteth the stumbling-block of his iniquity before his face, and cometh to the prophet, I, the Lord, will answer him that cometh according to the multitude of his idols; that I may take the house of Israel in their own heart."

Brother Joseph must have set up his idol in his heart, or he would not have prayed to the Lord to know wherein David and Solomon were justified in polygamy, when God says in the Book of Mormon that they were *not* justified in it; that it was abominable before Him. David, Solomon, Saul, and many chosen men of God, afterwards drifted into error and lost the spirit of God, and why not Joseph Smith? Will you answer? Was not Joseph Smith a man subject to like passions? Had you been with him as much as I was, and knew him as I knew him, you would also know that he could fall into error and transgression: but with all his weaknesses, I always did love him. No man was ever perfect but Christ. Uzziah fell into the snare of Satan, through pride, after serving God in humility for fifty-two years, (2. Chron. xxvi). "I have seen folly in the prophets of Samaria." (Jer. xxiii:13). "I have seen in the prophets a horrible thing," (Jer. xxiii:14). "The prophets prophesy falsely," (Jer. v:31). "For the sins of her prophets, and the iniquities of her priests," (Lam. iv: 13). "Thus saith the Lord, woe unto the foolish prophets," (Ezek. xiii:3). There were many prophets and chosen men of God, who afterwards fell into error, and who lost the Spirit of God, and produced false prophecies and revelations in the name of the Lord. Why should any one refuse to investigate as to the truth of the Book of Mormon, because Joseph Smith went into error after being called of God to translate it? Kind reader, think of this, and beware how you hastily condemn that book which I know to be the word of God; for his own voice and an angel from heaven declared the truth of it unto me, and to two other witnesses who testified on their death-bed that it was true. You say that angels do not appear unto men in these days, but the Word of God says: "Are they not all ministering spirits, sent forth to minister for them who shall be heirs of salvation?" (Heb. i:14.) There are now heirs of salvation upon earth, and I tell you of a truth that angels do minister unto them in these days. I hope the reader now understands this matter, viz: that no one who is seeking for truth honestly and without prejudice, will refuse to investigate the Book of Mormon because of Joseph Smith's errors. The teachings of the Book of Mormon are pure and holy, for it is the religion of Christ, set forth in plainness and simplicity.

I desire to say a few words especially to the Latter Day Saints who believe in the doctrine of polygamy. Why it is that you can put your trust in a man, and believe a revelation of his that contradicts the Word of God in the Book of Mormon, is very strange indeed. The revelation on polygamy begins thus: "Verily, thus saith the Lord unto you my servant Joseph, that inasmuch as you have inquired of my hand, to know wherein I the Lord, justified my servants Abraham, Isaac and Jacob; as also Moses, David and Solomon, my servants, as touching the principle and doctrine of their having many wives and concubines: * * * I will answer thee as touching this matter." The Book of Mormon says (Jacob ii:6): "David and Solomon truly had many wives and concubines, which thing was ABOMINABLE before me, saith the Lord." Then David and Solomon's polygamy was a great sin and an abomination before God. Joseph Smith's revelation says that it was NOT a sin, for it says that God JUSTIFIED David and Solomon in it!

So you see that revelation is a plain contradiction of the Word of God in the Book of Mormon. This is plain enough for any one to see and understand. Can you not see that this revelation is not of God? Why, oh why are you trusting in an arm of flesh? Again, the Book of Mormon says (page 116, Jacob ii:6), "Hearken to the word of the Lord: for there shall not any man among you have save it be one wife: and concubines he shall have none." In the face of this, you are believing in a revelation purporting to come from God, that He had changed and allowed his people to practice what He says *is a sin and an abomination in his sight!* Verily, you know not God nor his ways! Again, did Christ teach that a man is exalted to the highest glory hereafter through the principle of polygamy? Nay. The Book of Mormon says (1 Nephi iii:43), that all men must come to Christ "according to the words which shall be established by the mouth of (Christ) the Lamb: and the words of the Lamb shall be made known in the records of thy (Nephi's) seed, as well as in the records of the twelve apostles of the Lamb" (the New Testament). The revelations of Joseph Smith do not even claim to be translated from the sealed records of the Nephites. This alone should convince you that the revelation on polygamy *is not of God.* The scriptures say that if an angel from heaven preach any other gospel than that preached by Christ and his apostle, let him be accursed!

In the revelation on polygamy, it says that Emma Smith—Brother Joseph's wife—must receive the revelation to allow Brother Joseph to have more wives, or she shall be destroyed. But in less than a year after giving this revelation, Brother Joseph himself was destroyed, and Emma lived for many years after. I will quote it: "And let mine handmaid, Emma Smith, receive all those that have been given unto my servant Joseph. * * * * And I command mine handmaid, Emma Smith, to abide and cleave unto my servant Joseph, and to none else. But if she will not abide this commandment she shall be destroyed." You are blinded and cannot understand the scriptures. Many prophets of old were deceived by revelations which they thought were of God, but were of Satan, given to deceive and blind them and the people because of their iniquities. The decrees of God in the Book of Mormon are; that if his people who live upon this land obey the laws of God and the laws of the land, that they shall live in peace and prosperity; and their enemies should not have power over them. My soul cries unto you, repent! repent! and go to God in mighty prayer that he may open your hearts to see and understand that you are deceived in believing that the doctrine of polygamy is a revelation from God. I know there are many honest hearts among you, and I pray to God continually for those, that their eyes may be opened to understand the truth as it is in Christ.

CHAPTER V

ONE MAN TO LEAD AND RECEIVE REVELATIONS FOR THE CHURCH, NOT ACCORDING TO THE TEACHINGS OF CHRIST.

When Christ came into the world, the doctrine of a one-man leader to the church was not taught by him, and we are under his teachings in the written word. In the old covenant in the Book of Mormon is a prophecy that a "Choice Seer" is to come forth—of the seed of Joseph, of the seed of Lehi—who is to bring forth the word of the Lord from the sealed records of the Nephites, and convince the Lamanites, and restore them and the house of Israel; his work is not defined any farther than this. We suppose his work will be defined in the records which he will hereafter bring forth. We are told in 2 Nephi ii:17, Ether i:11, that the sealed records are not to come forth in the days of wickedness and abominations of the people. Then the more wicked part of the people will be cut off before they are brought forth. It may be as it was when Christ came to the people on this continent. We are told in Ether i:11, that the sealed records "shall not go forth unto the Gentiles until the day that they shall repent of their iniquity, and become clean before the Lord," and have faith in him even as the brother of Jared did. Again, it says this "Choice Seer" will do strictly according to the commandments of God. This means that he will be a holy man. We have seen from a revelation given to Brother Joseph, that he broke the commandments of God from the beginning. Now, as the wicked will be cut off, the people being clean before the Lord, and this Choice Seer being a holy man, the people in this condition will be fitted to give heed to him, and they will not be led astray by him, because the Word of God says so. At the present time we are under the teachings of Christ in the written word, and his teachings to us, the Book of Mormon plainly tells us, are to be made known in the records of the Jews (the Bible), and the Nephite records. "All men must come unto him, or they cannot be saved; AND THEY MUST COME ACCORDING TO THE WORDS WHICH SHALL BE ESTABLISHED BY THE MOUTH OF THE LAMB: AND THE WORDS OF THE LAMB SHALL BE MADE KNOWN IN THE RECORDS OF THY SEED (THE NEPHITE RECORDS), AS WELL AS IN THE RECORDS OF THE TWELVE APOSTLES OF THE LAMB (the Bible); wherefore they both shall be established in one." (1 Nephi iii:43.)

All men must come to Christ according to the words which shall be established by Christ, AND HIS WORDS SHALL BE MADE KNOWN IN THE NEPHITE RECORDS AND THE BIBLE. So the book of Doctrine and Covenants must be laid down. Brethren, this scripture is very plain, and I hope that none of you will attempt to wrest it to uphold the book of Doctrine and Covenants. Then let us heed only the teachings of Christ which we have, and discard the teachings of Joseph Smith or any other man or angel which conflict with Christ's teachings in the Bible and Book or Mormon: and when more of the words of Christ come forth in the way that it is appointed to come, from the sealed records, then we will heed it also.

There is nothing in the New Testament part of either the Bible or Book of Mormon concerning a one-man leader or head to the church. Whoever claims that such an office should be in the church to-day, goes beyond the teachings which Christ has given us. As I have stated, we were strictly commanded in the beginning to rely upon that which was written; and he who goes beyond that which was then written, to the revelations of Joseph Smith to establish any order or doctrine in the church, must come under the head of those whom Christ spoke of when he said, "Whosoever teaches more or less, etc., is not of me." This alone should satisfy anyone who is not trusting in an arm of flesh. Who was "Prophet Seer and Revelator" to the church at Jerusalem? They had none. Who was "Prophet Seer and Revelator" to the church upon this land? They had none. And we had no such an office in the church in these last days for the first eight months of its existence, until Brother Joseph went into this error on April 6, 1830, and, after unwittingly breaking a command of God by taking upon himself such an office, in a few years those revelations were changed to admit this high office, which otherwise would have condemned it. They were changed to mean something entirely different from the way they were first given and printed in the Book of Commandments; as if God had not thought of this great and important office when he gave those revelations. Yet in the face of the written word of God, and in the face of all this evidence, the majority of the Latter Day Saints will still cling to the revelations of Joseph Smith and measure the written word of God by them, instead of measuring Joseph Smith and his revelations by the written word. Speaking after the manner of Paul to the Galatians, so say I to you: O foolish Latter Day Saints * * * I marvel, that ye are so soon removed from him that called you into the grace of Christ, unto another gospel; which is not another, but the same gospel which some have perverted; and though we, or an angel from heaven, or Joseph Smith, preach any other gospel unto you than that which Christ gave us in the beginning, receive it not. (See Gal. i:6-9).

In the Church of Christ at Jerusalem, and upon this land, the members all received the revealed will of God for themselves, through the various gifts of the Holy Ghost; by dreams, visions, the visitation of Angels, the gift of prophecy, through themselves or any brother; and the Holy Ghost that was in them always discerning whether the revelation was of God or not. They had no Prophet Seer and Revelator to go to when they desired to know the will of the Lord concerning them; they went to the Lord themselves; sometimes alone, and sometimes several of them together in fasting and prayer. Of course I believe that God reveals his will to his servants in these last days, just as in days of old, but I believe in it according to the scriptures of divine truth.

In the Church upon the Eastern continent, after Christ had ascended to His Father's throne and left the work with his disciples to carry on, they went to God for themselves, each and all of them receiving the will of God by the various gifts of the Holy Ghost. Paul, Peter, Barnabas, Philip and others went here and there preaching, every one receiving revelations from God for themselves, by dreams, visions, the gift of prophecy, etc. They had no head of the Church on earth to go to. Christ told them that the Holy Ghost—the Comforter—that would abide with them and with all his disciples, would guide them and lead them into all truth and show them things to come. If any man lacks wisdom, and desires to know the will of the Lord concerning himself, *let him ask of God for himself,* not ask of the Prophet Seer and Revelator to inquire of the Lord for him.

Just after Christ had established his church upon this land and ascended into heaven, there were disputations among the Nephite brethren on one point; that was the name by which they must call the church. The brethren did not go to a Prophet Seer and Revelator to get him to inquire of the Lord about this matter; Christ had not so instructed them. They had no such an officer in the church. They went to God in prayer and fasting, and received an answer to their prayers, and it was not through any head or leader to the church, but Christ himself.

Brethren, this high office as you have it, is of far more importance than any other office in the church. Now do you not suppose that if Christ meant for such an office to be in the church to-day, that full instructions would have been given in his teachings about it? As you know we were commanded in the beginning to rely upon that which is written. Such an office in Christ's teachings in either book is not even mentioned; but I need not rehearse the matter. I cannot make it any more plain. As I have said, you have the scriptures before you, and if you will wrest them it shall be to your own destruction. This matter of a one-man mouthpiece of God to the church, has proven the great curse of the work of God in these last days. It is through this instrumentality that Satan has many thousand souls deluded. A man who was weak and unstable from the time God called him, set himself up as Prophet and Seer to the church, and the church to receive his words as if from God's own mouth. Such a thing is contrary to the Spirit and truths of our Lord Jesus Christ. Look at the one hundred and fifty thousand deluded souls in Utah, believing in a revelation given through this man that we are to exalted to the highest glory in the world to come, through spiritual wifeism; also the twenty thousand or more souls who are blinded to believe in the revelations of this man who has introduced doctrines into the church that conflict with the written word of God. As it was in the days of ancient Israel and in the days of the Apostles, so it is in this day. "Cursed be the man that trusteth in man and maketh flesh his arm, and whose heart departeth from the Lord." Jer. xvii:5.

CHAPTER VI

THE DOCTRINE OF CHRIST ALL CONTAINED IN THE TWO SACRED BOOKS.

Some of the Latter Day Saints have claimed that as the Book of Mormon is an abridgement of the Nephite records, it does not contain all the doctrine of Christ, hence the need of the revelations of Joseph Smith. All who make this claim are in error, as Christ himself says, (Nephi ix:11), that his doctrine is contained in the Book of Mormon. In speaking of the Book of Mormon he says, that when these things shall be made known unto the Gentiles, that they might "know of the true points of my doctrine." We have also see in the previous chapter, that the words and doctrine of Christ are to be made known in the Bible and in the Nephite records. Now brethren, these scriptures are as plain as can be; they need no comments of mine to make them any more plain. The Doctrine and Covenants do not claim to have been translated from the records of Nephi's seed—the sealed records. This plain scripture should and will be sufficient to convince any person without prejudice, that the Doctrine and Covenants should be discarded as a law of God to the church. The doctrine of Christ always was and will be the same. The Book of Mormon tells us that the sealed records yet to come forth will contain great mysteries of things that are to transpire before the end of the world; but this is another thing outside of the gospel or doctrine of Christ. Paul says that if an angel from heaven preach any other gospel unto you, let him be accursed. The teachings or doctrine of Christ as set forth in the Book of Mormon are full and plain. Mormon says, "and now there cannot be written in this book even the hundredth part of the things which Jesus did truly teach the people." Of course this means all the words that Jesus taught or spoke to them, including the great mysteries of things to take place in the future, which mysteries the Lord forbade them to write. John also says of the things which Jesus truly did and taught, "the which, if they should be written every one, I suppose that even the world itself could not contain the books that should be written." (John xxi:25). But is any one so blind as to understand from this language that the doctrine of Christ, or as we use the expression, the teachings of Christ, are not contained in full in the Bible and Book of Mormon? No spiritual man would so interpret this scripture.

In June, 1829, Joseph Smith, Oliver Cowdery and myself, received this commandment through the stone, "Behold, I give unto you a commandment, that you rely upon the things which are written (then, at that time, June, 1829), for in them are all things written concerning my church, my gospel, and my rock." This revelation reads this way to-day in the old Book of Commandments. But the Latter Day saints changed it in 1834 to read different in the Book of Doctrine and Covenants. The revelations received through the stone in 1829, agree with the teachings of Christ in the Bible and Book of Mormon; but in order to support the errors which were afterwards introduced by men, some of the early revelations have been changed and added to, as I will show you in another chapter. In order to uphold these errors, your leaders claim that as the Book of Mormon is an abridgement of the Nephite records, containing only a small part of the things which Christ said and did, that it does not contain all the doctrines, laws, ordinances and offices which Christ meant to be in the church; therefore Brother Joseph's revelations are needed to establish other doctrines, laws, ordinances and offices that Christ left out of the Book of Mormon and the Bible, and out of the revelations when God first gave them in 1829. Oh the weakness and folly of man! How any person can be so blind in the face of all this evidence, as to still uphold the Book of Doctrine and Covenants, is more than I can understand. But there are none so blind as those who will not see.

You have changed the revelations from the way they were first given and as they are to-day in the Book of Commandments, to support the error of Brother Joseph in taking upon himself the office of Seer to the church. You have changed the revelations to support the error of high priests. You have changed the revelations to support the error of a President of the high priesthood, high counselors, etc. You have altered the revelations to support you in going beyond the plain teachings of Christ in the new covenant part of the Book of Mormon. You have changed and altered the revelations to support the error of publishing those revelations in a book: the errors you are in, revelations have been changed to support and uphold them. You who are now living did not change them, but you who strive to defend these things, are as guilty in the sight of God as those who did change them.

As I have stated, I am called to bear testimony that the Bible, as well as the Book of Mormon, is true: and no one should place the one book ahead of the other; they are one! The Book of Mormon tells us that many plain things have been taken from the Bible, so that the Gentiles stumble and contend about the true points of Christ's doctrine. It says that the Book of Mormon has been kept pure, and come forth pure so as to make plain the doctrine of Christ; that we might know of the true points of his doctrine. Is it not plain that we should rely upon it on all doctrinal points, and the order of offices in the church? It certainly is, and this is not placing it ahead of the Bible. The Book of Mormon is full and plain on the doctrine of Christ. Christ chose "twelve" and called them disciples, or elders (not apostles); and the "twelve" ordained elders, priests, and teachers. These are all the spiritual offices in the church: that is, the officers who are ordained to officiate in spiritual ordinances; as baptism, laying on of hands for the gift of the Holy Ghost; ordaining other officers, administering the Lord's supper, etc. The office of a Bishop is to administer in temporal things. He is the business man of the church. The church has a right to appoint officers who act in a temporal capacity; this is outside of the spiritual offices. We see that the disciples at Jerusalem appointed temporal officers. Acts vi:2-3: "Then the twelve called the multitude of the disciples unto them, and said: It is not reason that we should leave the word of God and serve tables. Wherefore, brethren, look ye out among you seven men of honest report, full of the Holy Ghost and wisdom, whom we may appoint over this business." So they appointed the seven deacons.

"And God hath set some in the church, first apostles, secondarily prophets, thirdly teachers, after that miracles, then gifts of healings, helps, governments, diversities of tongues." (1 Cor. xii:28). The Latter Day Saints stumble over this passage, and it is strange that they do. Paul is not referring here to all the officers in the church. The office of an Elder is not named. He refers to miracles, gifts of healing, diversities of tongues, and these are not *offices* in the Church. He is referring here to the gifts, as you can see plainly by reading the chapter. He says at the conclusion of this, in the thirty-first verse, "But covet earnestly the best gifts." In the New Testament it speaks of evangelists, pastors, teachers, helps, governments, etc. Are we to suppose from this, that we are now to establish offices in the Church under those respective names of helps, pastors, governments, etc.? Not at all. These names come to us thus translated. Concerning the spiritual offices in the church, Elders, Priests and Teachers, with their duties as given in the Book of Mormon, they comprise the officers who are qualified to act in *all* spiritual matters, and there is no need of any more spiritual offices than these in the church, as we can plainly see from the scriptures.

The Book of Mormon is full concerning all spiritual matters pertaining to the Church of Christ. Instructions are given as to the manner of baptism, laying on of hands, the manner of administering the flesh and blood of Christ; that the church must meet together oft to fast and to pray and to speak concerning the welfare of their souls; how the meeting should be conducted; how a back-sliding member is to be tried, before the Elders by the testimony of three witnesses, and if they repented not, they were to be cut off, etc., etc. It is all set forth therein in plainness, and we have no need of the Doctrine and Covenants or any other creed.

The twelve at Jerusalem are called in the written word "Apostles." They are apostles because they were special witnesses to the sufferings of Christ, His death, burial and resurrection: but the twelve which Christ chose on this land are called disciples or elders, and are not once called apostles in the Book of Mormon. In the revelation which came through the stone in June, 1829, to Oliver Cowdery and myself to search out the twelve, they are also called disciples, and not apostles; and the revelation says "disciples" in the Book of Commandments to-day. But it has been changed in the Doctrine and Covenants to read "apostles." The heading to this revelation in the Book of Commandments says: "Making known the calling of twelve 'Disciples' in these last days." In the Doctrines and Covenants to reads: "Making known the calling of twelve 'Apostles' in these last days." In 1 Nephi iii:26, where reference is made to the twelve at Jerusalem and the twelve upon this land, each twelve are called by their respective names: "Behold the twelve 'Disciples' of the Lamb, who are chosen to minister unto thy seed. And he (the angel) said unto me, thou remembereth the twelve 'Apostles' of the Lamb? Behold they are they who shall judge the twelve tribes of Israel: wherefore, the twelve ministers of thy seed shall be judged of them." The twelve on this land are called disciples, and not in any place are they called apostles. When Christ was teaching the twelve on this land, in giving them instructions He refers to the way His twelve apostles did at Jerusalem in the laying on of hands, saying to them: "For thus do mine apostles."

In 1 Cor. xii:28, it says: "And God hath set some in the church, first apostles, secondarily prophets," etc. He did so, placing the twelve apostles first, which he chose at Jerusalem: they are to judge the twelve tribes of Israel, and they are to judge the twelve disciples whom Christ chose on this land among the Nephites. Therefore, we see from the written word that there is only one twelve who are called apostles, and that they are placed first.

When it is God's own due time to gather up the scattered fragments of his kingdom which has been laid waste by men, then we suppose that God will place at the head of his church twelve disciples; but we of the Church of Christ will not place them there, unless God so commands us. This is God's work and not man's work. We do not believe in twelve man-made disciples.

I consider the Book of Doctrine and Covenants a creed of religious faith. You can see from the first edition (Kirtland, 1835) that men, on the authority of other men, and no authority from God, "arranged the items of the doctrine of Jesus Christ" in that book, and in August, 1835, adopted it as the doctrine and covenants of their faith by a unanimous vote of the high council, thus making it a law to the church for the first time. To these proceedings I objected from the first, as I also did to changing the name of the church. Why should they not have been satisfied with the way that God has arranged the items of his doctrine in his Holy Word? What authority had they for making a creed? I will quote from the Kirtland edition of the Book of Doctrine and Covenants of 1835, and you can see for yourselves that what I say is correct. Quotation from the preface: "We deem it to be unnecessary to entertain you with a lengthy preface to the following volume, but merely to say that it contains in short the leading items of the religion which we have professed to believe. The first part of the book will be found to contain a series of lectures as delivered before a theological class in this place, and, in consequence of their embracing the important doctrine of salvation, we have arranged them into the following work. * * * There may be an aversion in the minds of some against receiving anything purporting to be articles of religious faith, in consequence of there being so many CREEDS now extant; but if men believe a system and profess that it was given by inspiration, certainly the more intelligibly they can present it the better. * * * We have, therefore, endeavored to present, though in few words, OUR belief, and, when we say this, humbly trust the faith and principles of this society as a body."

Where is their authority from God for making this creed, and making it a law to the church? I will now quote from pages 255 and 256 of the same book: "The assembly being duly organized, and, after transacting certain business of the church, proceeded to appoint a committee to ARRANGE THE ITEMS OF DOCTRINE OF JESUS CHRIST. * * * These items are to be taken from the Bible, Book of Mormon, and the revelations which have been given to said church up to its date, or shall be until such arrangement is made. * * * Whereupon the High Council of

Kirtland accepted and acknowledged them as the doctrine and covenants of their faith by a unanimous vote." It was here made a law to the church for the first time. So we see that their whole proceedings were upon their own authority—upon the authority of men and not God. Also, that the Doctrine and Covenants is a creed, as much so as any sectarian creed.

Some of the Latter Day Saints claim that the Doctrine and Covenants is one of the Books spoken of in Nephi's vision, which he saw taken to the Lamanites from the Gentiles. (1 Nephi iii:42.) How anyone can so interpret that scripture is more than I can understand; because it says on the same page, that those "Books" (records) contained the words that Christ spake unto the Nephites, which words should be hid up, to come forth to the Gentiles, after the Nephites had dwindled in unbelief. Nephi saw "other Books" taken to the Lamanites, after the Bible was taken to them. The Book of Mormon is one of those books, but the other is yet to come forth from the Nephite records, which are yet hid up and sealed. It is to come to the Gentiles, and they will carry it and the Book of Mormon to the Lamanites, to the convincing of the Gentiles, the Lamanites and the Jews. Now, how is it that anyone can claim the Doctrine and Covenants as being one of those "Books"? The Book of Doctrine and Covenants itself does not claim to be the words of the Nephite record which are hid up. The Book of Mormon was translated from those records, and more is yet to be translated from them, but it will not come forth in the days of wickedness (2 Nephi xi:17. Ether i:11). I will quote the scripture relating to the "other Books" which Nephi saw in his vision. It is very plain. (1 Nephi iii:41-42). The angel, talking to Nephi, says: "Behold, saith the Lamb, I will manifest myself unto thy seed (the Nephites), that they shall write many things which I shall minister unto them, which shall be plain and precious; and after thy seed shall be destroyed and dwindle in unbelief, and also the seed of thy brethren; behold, these things shall be hid up, to come forth unto the Gentiles, by the gift and power of the Lamb; and in them shall be written my gospel, saith the Lamb, and my rock and my salvation; * * * * (same page) And it came to pass that I beheld the remnant of the seed of my brethren (the Lamanites), and also the Book of the Lamb of God, which had proceeded forth from the mouth of the Jew (the Bible), that it came forth from the Gentiles, unto the remnant of the seed of my brethren; and after it had come forth unto them (the Lamanites), I beheld OTHER BOOKS, which came forth by the power of the Lamb, from the Gentiles unto them, unto the convincing of the Gentiles, and the remnant of the seed of my brethren, and also the Jews, who were scattered upon all the face of the earth," etc.

Now brethren, words cannot be plainer than this scripture, and it shows that the Book of Doctrine and Covenants is not one of those books. It is strange to me, why the heads of your church will attempt to prove that the Book of Doctrine and Covenants is one of those books here spoken of, as they are to come from sealed records which are yet hid up.

CHAPTER VII

RELATIVE TO PUBLISHING THE REVELATIONS.

Publishing the early revelations, or any of them, was contrary to the will of the Lord, as I will show you from the revelations themselves. The revelations in the Book of Commandments up to June, 1829, were given through the "stone," through which the Book of Mormon was translated. These are the only revelations that can be relied upon, and they are not law. The Lord told us not to teach them for doctrine; they were given mostly to individuals, the persons whom God chose in commencing His work for their individual instruction, and the church had no need of them. They should have been kept with the sacred papers and records of the church, and never published in a book to become public property for the eyes of the world. It was not necessary for the whole church to ever see them. The written word is full on all matters pertaining to the Church of Christ. Of course I believe in God revealing His will to His servants in these days, by the various gifts of the Holy Ghost; but I believe in it according to the Scriptures. In the revelations themselves are positive commands to keep these things from the world, that they are sacred, etc. A revelation was given to Oliver Cowdery in April, 1829, (Sec. v:11, 13), in which he is told that he would be granted a gift "to translate even as my servant Joseph," warning him as follows: "Remember, it is sacred, and cometh from above." * * * * "Trifle not with sacred things." * * * * "Make not thy gift known unto any, save it be those who are of thy faith." But they published these things in a book, and made them known to the world!

In a revelation to Martin Harris (Sec. 18) concerning endless punishment, are these words: "And I command you that you preach naught but repentance; and show not these things, neither speak these things unto the world, for they cannot bear meat, but milk they must receive: wherefore, they must not know these things, lest they perish." This revelation reads as I have quoted it, in the Book of Commandments; but in the Doctrine and Covenants it has been changed to read thus: "Show not these things unto the world, until it is wisdom in me." The words, "until it is wisdom in me," were added to this revelation. You see they had to add these words in order to publish the revelations. Judge for yourselves, brethren: I will make no farther comments to magnify the errors of the leaders of the church. My policy throughout will be to speak of no more of their errors than is necessary in order to prove all false doctrines as being false, and establishing the doctrine of Christ as it is set forth in the written word.

The main reason why the printing press was destroyed, was because they published the Book of Commandments. It fell into the hands of the world, and the people of Jackson county, Missouri, saw from the revelations that they were considered by the church as intruders upon the land of Zion, as enemies to the church, and that they should be cut off out of the land of Zion and sent away. The people seeing these things in the Book of Commandments became the more enraged, tore down the printing press, and drove the church out of Jackson county. (See Doc. and Cov., Sections 52:9, 64:7, 45:15.) "Which is the land of your inheritance. Which is now the land of your enemies." "And the rebellious shall be cut off out of the land of Zion, and shall be sent away, and shall not inherit the land." "And now I say unto you, keep these things from going abroad unto the world, until it is expedient in me, that ye may accomplish this work in the eyes of the people, and in the eyes of your enemies, that they may not know your works until ye have accomplished the thing which I have commanded you." This is sufficient. I will quote no more to show you that the leaders made a mistake in publishing the revelations in a book. It is too plain.

Brethren, does it not look strange that they should have been so blind as to go ahead and publish these revelations in the face of this plain language to keep these things from the world? It surely does look strange.

I will now tell you of a prophecy which the Lord gave through me to Brothers Joseph Smith and Sydney Rigdon, of what should come to pass if they printed those revelations. In the spring of 1832, in Hiram, Ohio, Brothers Joseph and Sydney, and others, concluded that the revelations should be printed in a book. A few of the brethren—including myself—objected to it seriously. We told them that if the revelations were published, the world would get the books, and it would not do; that it was not the will of the Lord that the revelations should be published. But Brothers Joseph and Sydney would not listen to us, and said they were going to send them to Independence to be published. I objected to it and withstood Brothers Joseph and Sydney to the face. Brother Joseph said as follows: "Any man who objects to having these revelations published, shall have his part taken out of the Tree of Life and out of the Holy City." The Spirit of God came upon me and I prophesied to them in the name of the Lord: "That if they sent those revelations to Independence to be published in a book, the people would come upon them and tear down the printing press, and the church would be driven out of Jackson county." Brothers Joseph and Sydney laughed at me. Early in the spring of 1833, at Independence, Mo., the revelations were printed in the Book of Commandments. Many of the books were finished and distributed among the members of the church, and through some of the unwise brethren, the world got hold of some of them. From that time the ill-feeling toward us began to increase; and in the summer of 1833 the mob came upon us, tore down the printing press, and drove the church out of Jackson county. Brothers Joseph and Sydney then saw that I did have some of the Spirit of God, after my prophecy had been fulfilled. To show you that Brother Joseph and myself still loved each other as brethren after this, I will tell you that he had so much confidence in me that in July, 1834, he ordained me his successor as "Prophet Seer and Revelator" to the Church. He did this of his own free will and not at any solicitation whatever on my part. I did not know what he was going to do until he laid his hands upon me and ordained me.

Now, bear in mind, brethren, that I am not claiming this office; as I have told you, I do not believe in any such an office in the church. I was then in error in believing that there was such an office in the Church of Christ. I suppose this is news to many of you—that Brother Joseph ordained me his successor—but it is in your records, and there are men now living who were present in that council of elders when he did it, in the camp of Zion, on Fishing River, Missouri, July, 1834.

This is why many of the brethren came to me after Brother Joseph was killed, and importuned me to come out and lead the church. I refused to do so. *Christ* is the only leader and head of his church.

Now, brethren, I will ask you to read the early revelations that were given through the stone, up to June, 1829, and see if this matter is not just as I have told you; that they—or any other revelations—should never have been published, thus necessarily becoming public property for the eyes of the world. Also notice that they were given to individuals, to those whom God chose in commencing his work, for their individual instruction, and were not given to the church, and the church had no need of them. In the Book of Doctrine and Covenants they are sections 2 to 16, inclusive. The headings over sections 4 and 7 are not like they are in the Book of Commandments, in which the headings show that they were also given to individuals. Section 4 is a revelation given to Joseph Smith and Martin Harris. Section 7 is a revelation given to Oliver Cowdery.

Now, bear in mind that these revelations were given through the "stone," while the Book of Mormon was being translated. The revelations in June, 1829, were given about the time the translation of the book was finished. As I have stated before, Brother Joseph gave up the stone a few months after translating the Book of Mormon. You can see from the Book of Doctrine and Covenants that the next revelation after June, 1829, is March, 1830, a period of nine months, and we had been preaching since August, 1829. Now you notice that when the revelations began to come again, at the end of this nine months (this time through Brother Joseph as "mouthpiece"), they came thick and fast, and are of a different character to those given through the stone, which were given to individuals for their individual instruction in commencing the work.

CHAPTER VIII

THE CHANGES AND ADDITIONS TO SOME OF THE REVELATIONS.

Some of the revelations as they are now in the Book of Doctrine and Covenants have been changed and added to. Some of the changes being of the greatest importance as the meaning is entirely changed on some very important matters; as if the Lord had changed his mind a few years after he gave the revelations, and after having commanded his servants (as they claim) to print them in the "Book of Commandments;" and after giving his servants a revelation, being a preface until His Book of Commandments, which says: "Behold, this is mine authority, and the authority of my servants, and my preface unto the Book of my Commandments, which I have given them to publish unto you, oh inhabitants of the earth." Also in this preface, "Behold, I am God, and have spoken it; these commandments are of me." "Search these commandments, for they are true and faithful." The revelations were printed in the Book of Commandments correctly. This I know, and will prove it to you.

These revelations were arranged for publication by Brothers Joseph Smith, Sydney Rigdon, Orson Hyde and others, in Hiram, Ohio, while I was there, were sent to Independence to be published, and were printed just exactly as they were arranged by Brother Joseph and the others. And when the Book of Commandments was printed, Joseph and the church received it as being printed correctly. This I know. In the winter of 1834 they saw that some of the revelations in the Book of Commandments *had to be changed*, because the heads of the church had gone too far, and had done things in which they had already gone ahead of some of the former revelations. So the book of "Doctrine and Covenants" was printed in 1835, and some of the revelations changed and added to. By the providence of God I have one of the old Book of Commandments published in 1833. I will prove by a revelation in it, which is changed in the Doctrine and Covenants, a revelation that was given through the "stone" and is true—I will prove that God called Brother Joseph to translate the Book of Mormon only, and that he was not called to organize and establish the church any more than the rest of us Elders. That God commanded him that he should pretend to no other gift but to translate the Book of Mormon, that God would grant him no other gift.

I will also show by a revelation in the Book of Commandments—afterwards changed in the Doctrine and Covenants—that we were commanded to rely upon the "things which are written" in building up the church; for "in them are all things written concerning my church, my gospel, and my rock. Wherefore, if you shall build up *my* church, *my* gospel, and *my* rock, the gates of hell shall not prevail against you." But we did not rely upon the written word in building up the church; but Joseph went *"on in the persuasions of men,"* —as he did while translating, and heeded Rigdon who showed him that high priests and other offices should be added to "elders, priests and teachers;" and so we did not establish *His* (Christ's) church, *His* gospel and *His* rock, so the gates of hell *did* prevail against the church, and it finally landed in Salt Lake in polygamy.

I will also show you by a revelation in the Book of Commandments—afterwards changed in the Doctrine and Covenants—that we had no high priests, etc. in the beginning; as if God had organized his church at first with "elders, priests and teachers," and after we had preached almost two years, and had baptized and confirmed about 2000 souls into the Church of Christ, then God concluded he had not organized it right, and decided to put in high priests and other offices above the office of an elder. No brethren—God does not change and work in any such manner. This is *man's* work. I will prove beyond a doubt that every spiritual office added to the church which is not according to the teachings of Christ to the "twelve" on this land, is the work of man, and not the work of God.

I see that some of you claim that the same power which gave these revelations, had authority to change them, and refer to Jer. xxxvi:32. By reading this passage you will see that the words which were added were *"like words;"* words which conveyed the same meaning—were added to that book by Jeremiah when he was writing it over again, because it had been burned in the fire by the king. But the words added to the two former revelations are *not "like words,"* as they change and reverse the original meaning: as if God had commanded Joseph to pretend to no other gift but to translate the Book of Mormon, that he would *"grant him no other gift,"* and then afterwards God had changed his mind and concluded to grant him another gift. God does not change and work in this manner. The way this revelation has been changed, twenty-two words being added to it, it would appear that God had broken His word after giving His word in plainness; commanding Brother Joseph to pretend to no other gift but to translate the Book of Mormon, and then the Lord had changed and concluded to grant Joseph the gift of a Seer to the Church.

This part of this revelation in the Book of Commandments reads thus: "And he (Joseph) has a gift to translate the Book and I have commanded him that he shall pretend to no other gift, for I will grant him no other gift."

But in the Doctrine and Covenants it has been changed and reads thus:

"And you have a gift to translate the plates, *and this is the first gift that I bestowed upon you,* and I have commanded you that you should pretend to no other gift, *until my purpose is fulfilled in this;* for I will grant unto you no other gift *until it is finished".*

May God have mercy on the heads of the church for their transgression is my prayer.

This revelation is Section 4, Doctrine and Covenants: Chap. 4, Book of Commandments.

The next important change I will speak of, is made in a revelation which was given to Brothers Joseph Smith, Oliver Cowdery, and myself in Fayette, New York, June, 1829. I was present when Brother Joseph received it through the stone. It is Chapter 15 Book of Commandments, Sec. 16 Doctrine and Covenants. In the Book of Commandments it reads thus.

"Behold I give unto you a commandment, that you rely upon the things which are written; for in them are all things written, concerning my church, my gospel, and my rock. Wherefore if you shall build up my church, and my gospel, and my rock, the gates of hell shall not prevail against you."

But in the Book of Doctrine and Covenants it has been changed and reads thus: "Behold I give unto you a commandment, that you rely upon the things which are written; for in them are all things written, concerning *'the foundation of'* my church, my gospel, and my rock; wherefore, if you shall build up my church *'upon the foundation of'* my gospel and my rock, the gates of hell shall not prevail against you."

The change in this revelation is of great importance; the word "them" refers to the plates—the Book of Mormon: We were commanded to rely upon it in building up the church; that is, in establishing *the doctrine, the order of offices,*etc.: "FOR IN THEM ARE ALL THINGS WRITTEN CONCERNING MY CHURCH, my gospel, and my rock." But this revelation has been changed by man to mean as follows: That therein is *not* all things written concerning the church, but only all things concerning *"the foundation of"* the church—or the beginning of the church: that you must build up the church, beginning according to the written word, and add new offices, new ordinances, and new doctrines as I (the Lord) reveal them to you from year to year: As a Seer to the Church; High Priests; Three of the First Presidency; Baptism for the Dead; Polygamy, etc., etc. When the Book of Doctrine and Covenants was compiled in 1834, the church had then received many revelations to establish new offices and doctrines that are not even mentioned in the New Covenant of either of the two sacred books. They changed this revelation in order to sustain these new doctrines: If they had not made this change, the plain language of the original revelation would have condemned the Book of Doctrine and Covenants. I want to repeat that I was present when Brother Joseph received this revelation through the stone: I am one of the persons to whom it was given, therefore I know of a surety that it was changed when printed in the Doctrine and Covenants in 1834. Likewise, concerning all these changes of which I will speak, I know that these changes were made. I was present when nearly all the early revelations were received. There are several of the old Books of Commandments yet in the land; bring them to light and see for yourselves that these revelations were changed just as I tell you.

These changes were made by the leaders of the church, who had drifted into error and spiritual blindness. Through the influence of Sydney Rigdon, Brother Joseph was led on and on into receiving revelations every year, to establish offices and doctrines which are not even mentioned in the teachings of Christ in the written word. In a few years they had gone away ahead of the written word, so that they had to change these revelations, as you will understand when I have finished.

The next important change I will notice, is in a revelation given to Martin Harris, March, 1830, (Chap. 16 Book of Commandments, Sec. 18 Doctrine and Covenants). In the Book of Commandments it reads thus: "And I command you that you preach nought but repentance; and show not these things unto the world, for they cannot bear meat, but milk they must receive: Wherefore, they must not know these things lest they perish."

But in the Book of Doctrines and Covenants it has been changed and reads as follows:

"And I command you that you preach nought but repentance, and show not these things unto the world, *'until it is wisdom in me,'* etc." The words *"until it is wisdom in me"* have been added.

As I have stated in the previous chapter, you can readily see why they made this change.

The next change of importance is in a revelation given in Fayette, New York, June, 1830. It was not given through the stone. (Chap. 4., Book of Commandments, Sec. 17, Doctrine and Covenants). The change or addition to this revelation is of such a bold character, that the compilers of the Book of Doctrine and Covenants put it in that book without the heading, which is over it in the Book of Commandments, which heading shows it to be a revelation. They have put it in the Doctrine and Covenants as "Section 17," but it is a revelation. The old church papers speak of it as a revelation, and the heading in the Book of Commandments shows that it is a revelation. I was present when Brother Joseph gave this revelation.

The heading over it in the Book of Commandments is as follows: *"The Articles and Covenants of the Church of Christ, given in Fayette, New York, June, 1830."* Two paragraphs have been added to it, having been thrust into the middle of it: Paragraphs 16 and 17 is the part added, which part speaks of high priests and other high offices that the church never knew of until almost two years after its beginning: As if God had made a mistake in the first organization of the church, and left out these high important offices which are all above an elder; and as if God had made a mistake and left these high offices out of that revelation when it was first given. Oh the weakness and blindness of man! This revelation as it is in the Book of Commandments, speaks of the duties of all the spiritual officers in the church; of elders, priests and teachers; but does not mention a word about the office of high priest, president of the high priesthood, high counselors, etc. The part added to this revelation was put there to give the duties of these high officers in ordinations. I repeat that the church never heard of or thought of having in it any of these offices, until we moved to Kirtland, Ohio, in the days of Sidney Rigdon. The Church of Christ upon either continent had no such offices in it, and Christ told us through the stone that he would establish his church "LIKE UNTO THE CHURCH WHICH WAS TAUGHT BY MY DISCIPLES IN THE DAYS OF OLD." * * * "If the people of this generation harden not their hearts." (Chap. 4., Par. 5, Book of Commandments).

Now brethren, the Church of Christ of old had in it only elders, priests and teachers; but the Church of Latter Day Saints, with its many new offices, doctrines, and ordinances which were not in the Church of Christ of old, is a very different church—a different order throughout. This is plain to be seen. Why, oh why will you continue to trust in the man who has erred and introduced doctrines of error into the Church of Christ? Why will you continue in blindness? But modern Israel is no better than ancient Israel. Man will not walk humbly before God and abide in his ordinances, although he has given them his word in great plainness. You are in spiritual blindness and you know it not.

I will now quote the two paragraphs which have been added to the revelation above mentioned:

"No person is to be ordained to any office in this church, where there is a regularly organized branch of the same, without the vote of that church; but the presiding elders, traveling bishops, high counselors, high priests and elders, may have the privilege of ordaining, where there is no branch of the church, that a vote may be called. Every president of the high priesthood (or presiding elder), bishop, high counselor and high priest, is to be ordained by the direction of a high council, or general conference."

In all the teachings of Christ, these high offices are not even mentioned as being in the Church of Christ.

There are other changes in this revelation, but this is the only change of importance.

The next change I will notice is one of importance. It is in Section 4, Doctrine and Covenants: Chapter 4, Book of Commandments. Half of a page has been left out of this revelation. I believe that the object of those who left it out was to strike out the following words:

"And thus, if the people of this generation harden not their hearts, I will work a reformation among them, and I will put down all lyings, etc., * * * * and I will establish my church, LIKE UNTO THE CHURCH WHICH WAS TAUGHT BY MY DISCIPLES IN THE DAYS OF OLD." They knew that the order of offices in the Church of Latter Day Saints, was *not* like the order in the Church of Christ of old; because the Church of Christ of old had in it only elders, priests and teachers: so they left out this part of the revelation when they published the Book of Doctrine and Covenants.

There are many other changes in the revelations, but I will not take the space and time to speak of any more of them.

I want to tell the brethren, that when the Book of Doctrine and Covenants was published, and presented to the church assembly in Kirtland, Ohio, in August, 1835, as recorded in the old church papers, a very few of the brethren then knew about most of the important changes that had been put in the Book of Doctrine and Covenants. In time it was generally found out, and the result was that some of the members left the church on account of it. A few members dissented from the church as early as 1832, on account of the spiritual blindness of some of the leaders. When it became generally known that these important changes had been made in the Doctrine and Covenants, many of the brethren objected seriously to it, but they did not want to say much for the sake of peace, as it was *Brother Joseph* and *the leaders* who did it. The majority of the members—poor weak souls—thought that anything *Brother Joseph* would do, must be all right; so in their blindness of heart, trusting in an arm of flesh, they looked over it and were led into error, and finally all talk about it ceased. I was told that Sidney Rigdon was the cause of those changes being made: by smooth talk he convinced Brother Joseph and that committee that it was all right.

The editors of the old church papers, *Evening and Morning Star* and *Messenger and Advocate*, admit that some changes were made in some of the revelations; that they added some items to some revelations, from other revelations. I will not accuse those who did it of being fully aware of the grievous error they were making when they added those items—that is, made those changes; I would rather believe that they were spiritually blinded when they did it: and that Satan deceived them, whispering to them that it was all right and acceptable unto God.

Some of the Latter Day Saints have claimed that God had the same right to authorize Brother Joseph to add to any revelations certain words and facts, that He had to give him any revelations at all: but only those who are trusting in an arm of flesh and are in spiritual blindness, would pretend to make this claim; that God would give his servants some revelations, command them to publish them in His Book of Commandments, and then authorize them to change and add to them some words which change and reverse the original meaning: as if God had changed his mind after giving his word. No brethren! God does not change and work in any such manner as this; all those who believe that God does work this way, my prayer for them is that they may repent, for they are in utter spiritual blindness.

I want to say a few words here in regard to section 17, in the Doctrine and Covenants. This revelation was published in the *"Evening and Morning Star"* in 1832, before the Book of Commandments was published, and was put in that paper as, "The Articles and Covenants of the Church of Christ, with a few items from other revelations." This revelation was received in June, 1830, and these two paragraphs were added in June, 1832, in that paper. Now I will explain why they did not print this revelation in the Book of Commandments in 1833, with these added parts in it. It is this: The heads of the church had not yet become sufficiently blinded to change a revelation that was given in 1830, and print it changed in God's Book of Commandments in 1833. W. W. Phelps is the one who printed this revelation in that paper with the "items" (Paragraphs 16 and 17), added to it; but when the heads of the church changed the name of the church to "The Church of Latter Day Saints," (leaving out the name of "Christ" entirely) when they did this, and compiled the Doctrine and Covenants in 1835, God had then given them over to blindness of mind, and they could print this revelation in God's book, as also other revelations, *changed and added to* with a *clear conscience,* as they did many other grievous things with a clear conscience after this, thinking they were all right. I have no doubt that Brother Joseph thought his works up to the time of his repentance just before his death, were acceptable unto God. Poor Joseph! He was blinded and became ensnared by proud, ambitious men. I labored hard with him to get him to see it—from 1835—and God alone knows the grief and sorrow I have had over it. I have been told that Joseph repented just before he died. He is in the hands of a just God. If David of old could obtain salvation by repentance, so could Brother Joseph Smith.

CHAPTER IX

HIGH PRIESTS.

High Priests were only in the church before Christ; and to have this office in the "Church of Christ" is not according to the teachings of Christ in either of the sacred books: Christ himself is our great and last High Priest. Brethren—I will tell you one thing which alone should settle this matter in your minds; it is this: you cannot find in the New Testament part of the Bible or Book of Mormon where one single high priest was ever in the Church of Christ. The office of an Elder is spoken of in many many places, but not one word about a High Priest being in the church. This alone should convince any one, and will convince any one who is without prejudice, that the office of High Priests was established in the church almost two years after its beginning by men who had drifted into error. You must admit that the church which was to be established in this dispensation, must be "like unto the church which was taught by Christ's disciples of old." Then the Church of Latter Day Saints is unlike the Church of Christ of old, because you have the office of High Priests in the church. The office of a High Priest as you have it, is of more importance than the office of an Elder; then why is not something said about this high office being in the Church which Christ came on earth to establish at Jerusalem and upon this land? Why is there not something said about this important office, and so much said about an Elder?

Brethren, it is strange—very strange—that you will continue to cling to the man, Joseph Smith, and measure the written word of God by his revelations. So has it been in all ages past. You are in spiritual blindness. *Hearing ye shall hear and shall not understand; seeing ye shall see and not perceive.* And this too when Christ has given us the Book of Mormon with the plain and precious things therein.

When Christ came into the world upon this land, Nephi was a great High Priest who had done many mighty works. Now Nephi had to lay down his robe of a High Priest just outside the door and come into the Church of Christ by baptism, to the office of an Elder, and not once after that is Nephi called a High Priest. At this time the Church of Christ was established upon this land. Christ comes into the world and preaches to them as he had to those at Jerusalem, giving them instructions concerning his Church and the New Covenant which he made with them, as he had with those on the eastern continent, telling them they were no longer under the old law of Moses, but from that time were under him. He chooses twelve disciples who were called Elders, to minister unto that people, and after giving them full instructions concerning the establishing of his church, he ascends into heaven. Elders, Priests and Teachers were ordained in his church, and full instructions given concerning their duties. Christ told his disciples to write his teachings, for they were to be hid up to come down to us as his teachings to us. Now this being the case, why are not some instructions given in the new covenant of that book concerning the office of High Priests? Of course there was no such an office in the Church of Christ upon this land, nor in the Church of Christ upon the eastern continent, nor should there be such an office in the Church to-day. It is a grievous sin to have such an office in the church. As well might you add to the teachings of Christ—circumcision—offering up the sacrifice of animals—or break the ordinances of Christ in any other way by going back to the old law of Moses.

We will now go to the New Testament in the Bible. In no place therein does it mention one single High Priest as being in the Church of Christ. High Priests are spoken of in Hebrews iv to ix, but only to explain that Jesus Christ is our great High Priest after the order of Melchisedec. It speaks of High Priests that offered up sacrifices under the old law, showing that Christ himself was after that order, but not once does it speak of the office of a High Priest continuing after Christ, except only in Christ himself; He being "the Apostle and High Priest of our profession; * * * our great High Priest that has passed into the heavens; * * * a Priest forever after the order of Melchisedec." "Seeing then that we have a great High Priest (and the only one) * * * let us come boldly unto the throne of grace, that we may obtain mercy, etc." This being the fulfillment of the old order of High Priests which was a type of Christ's order. Before Christ, the people came to the High Priest for mercy and forgiveness, through him offering up sacrifices for their sins; but now the people have the great High Priest even Jesus Christ to go to "that we may obtain mercy and find grace to help in time of need:" He having offered up his body a sacrifice for the sins of the world. "And having an High Priest over the house of God, let us draw near with a true heart in full assurance of faith," etc. This matter is plainly set forth in Hebrews, iv chapter.

Brethren, it is solemn mockery before God to have established in the church to-day this important office of which Christ alone is worthy. The office of Elder is spoken of all through the New Testament as being in the church, but not one High Priest; then of course they had no High Priests in the church upon the eastern continent.

Now Brethren, seeing they had no High Priests in the church of Christ of old, and none in the church of Christ in these last days until almost two years after its beginning—when the leaders began to drift into error; remembering the fact of the revelation being changed two years after it was given to include High Priests; taking these things into consideration, how is it that any one can say that the office of High Priest should be in the church of Christ to-day? I can account for it only on the grounds of your spiritual blindness. This matter is so plain and self-evident that any one should see and understand it. Brethren, your blindness must be utter blindness. May God have mercy on you is my prayer.

In no place in the word of God does it say that an Elder is after the order of Melchisedec, or after the order of the Melchisedec Priesthood. An Elder is after the order of Christ. This matter of "priesthood," since the days of Sydney Rigdon, has been the great hobby and stumbling-block of the Latter Day Saints. Priesthood means authority; and authority is the word we should use. I do not think the word priesthood is mentioned in the New Covenant of the Book of Mormon. Authority is the word we used for the first two years in the church—until Sydney Rigdon's days in Ohio. This matter of the two orders of priesthood in the Church of Christ, and lineal priesthood of the old law being in the church, all originated in the mind of Sydney Rigdon. He explained these things to Brother Joseph in his way, out of the old Scriptures, and got Brother Joseph to inquire, etc. He would inquire, and as mouthpiece speak out the revelations just as they had it fixed up in their hearts. As I have said before, according to the desires of the heart, the inspiration comes, but it may be the spirit of man that gives it. How easily a man can receive some other spirit, appearing as an Angel of Light, believing at the time that he is giving the revealed will of God; a doubt never entering his mind but what he is doing God's will. Of course I believe that Brother Joseph gave every revelation—including the one on polygamy—in all good conscience before God. This is the way the High Priests and the "priesthood" as you have it, was introduced into the Church of Christ almost two years after its beginning—and after we had baptized and confirmed about two thousand souls into the church.

When the Church of Christ was established at Jerusalem, and upon this continent, and in 1829, the officers which were to be in the church were made known *at its beginning,* and not two years afterwards.

In Kirtland, Ohio, in June, 1831, at a conference of the church, the first High Priests were ordained into the church. Brother Joseph ordained Lyman Wight, John Murdock, Harvey Whitlock, Hyrum Smith, Reynolds Cahoon and others to the office of a High Priest. When they were ordained, right there at the time, the devil caught and bound Harvey Whitlock so he could not speak, his face being twisted into demon-like shape. Also John Murdock and others were caught by the devil in a similar manner. Now brethren, do you not see that the displeasure of the Lord was upon their proceedings in ordaining High Priests? Of course it was. These facts are recorded in the History of the Church—written by my brother, John Whitmer, who was the regularly appointed church historian. I was not at that conference, being then in Hiram, which is near Kirtland, Ohio. I also have the testimony of Harvey Whitlock whom the devil caught and bound: also John Whitmer, who was present, and others who were present at the time, so I know it is true. John Whitmer wrote this in the church history when he was in full fellowship with the church. As a faithful historian he speaks of this matter, and tries to explain it away by saying, "While the Lord poured out his spirit, the devil took occasion to make his power known; he bound Harvey Whitlock so that he could not speak, and others were affected, but the Lord showed to Joseph the seer, the design of this thing: He commanded the devil in the name of Christ and he departed to our joy and comfort." It was not given to Brother John nor any of them at that time to understand this matter of the devil entering into the first High Priests that were ordained in the church. They were all blind as to the design of that thing, and did not see what it meant. Of course it was given to Brother Joseph to cast the devil out, but what was the design of the devil entering into these men just as soon as they were ordained the first High Priests ever ordained in the church? Of course it was to show that God's sore displeasure was upon their erring works of ordaining High Priests into the Church of Christ. Any spiritual man can see this. Brother John was himself ordained a High Priest at that time, so he was in error and could not see it; but he saw it very clearly in 1848, when the Lord opened our eyes to see and understand it. Prejudiced persons are blind and do not want to see and understand except *their own preconceived way.* There is none so blind as those who will not see. In Brother John's history he speaks of the Spirit of God being poured out in abundance upon that occasion, some seeing visions, etc., but brethren, you will learn in the next world, if you do not know it already, that the devil can give visions, appearing as an Angel of Light. Brother John gives an account of a prophecy uttered by Lyman Wight just after Brother Joseph ordained him a High Priest, which prophecy will prove to be a false prophecy. Brother John's history of the church says as follows: "He (Joseph) laid his hands upon Lyman Wight and ordained him to the high priesthood after the holy order of God. And the spirit fell upon Lyman, and he prophesied concerning the coming of Christ. He said that there were some in this congregation that should live until the Savior should descend from Heaven with a shout, with all the holy angels with him, etc." The early future will determine as to whether this prophecy was true or false.

Some of the brethren have gone outside of the written word of God, and accepted as evidence, histories that were written 350 to 400 years after Christ, to prove that High Priests were in the Church of Christ. This seems strange to me. They have quoted from the history of St. Jerome, who was Secretary to the Pope at Rome, about 382 years after Christ. I should not wonder if the apostolic church did have High Priests and many other offices and ordinances that were abominable before God, after they drifted into error like the Latter Day Saints have. They have also quoted from Theodoret who died 457 years after Christ. His writings extend from A.D. 325 to A.D. 429. My authority for the above is Lippincott's Biographical Dictionary. Now shall we take such evidence as this to prove the office of High Priests being in the church when it was in its purity, when the written word of God mentions all the church officers in many places and says nothing about a single High Priest? Nay verily. As for me, I must take the Scriptures for my authority. I cannot understand how any person can claim that an important office like High Priests should be, or was in the Church of Christ when it was in the true faith, when nothing is said in the Scriptures about it. The Scriptures were given by inspiration of God: and do you suppose that God would leave out of his word the great office of a High Priest, if they were to be in the Church of Christ? Of course not. It is charging God foolishly to believe that he would leave out of his word this office or any other office that he intended should be in his church.

Some of the brethren have referred to 1 Peter ii:5-9 and Rev. i:6 to prove that there were High Priests in the Church of Christ, but the word High Priest is not mentioned in either passage. These two passages are all they have referred to in the whole of the New Testament, and no passage can be found in the New Testament part of the Book of Mormon to refer to, because High Priests are not even mentioned therein. In the above two passages there is no reference whatever to this office. In 1 Peter ii:5, 9, Peter is addressing the whole church, and says, "Ye also, as lively stones are built up a spiritual house, an holy priesthood, to offer up spiritual sacrifices, acceptable to God by Jesus Christ; * * * * Ye are a chosen generation, a royal priesthood, an holy nation, a peculiar people, etc." How any person can pretend to claim that this passage refers to the office of High Priest, is more than I can understand. If it does, then every member of the church holds this office, because Peter is addressing the whole church as you can see from the first of his epistle. Of course there is no reference made here to this office.

Rev. i:6 reads as follows: "Unto him that loved us, and washed us from our sins in his own blood, and hath made us kings and priests unto God and his father; to him be glory and dominion forever and ever. Amen." This has no reference to the office of a High Priest. It refers to the time when we will be in the Spirit, and can say as John then said, he being in the Spirit, unto Jesus Christ who hath redeemed us and hath made us kings and priests unto God, to him be glory and dominion forever and ever. Amen.

Some of the brethren have misunderstood the Old Testament part of the Book of Mormon concerning High Priests, and refer to Alma 9-6: Alma says, "This high priesthood being after the order of his Son, which order was from the foundation of the world: or in other words, being without beginning of days or end of years, being prepared from eternity to all eternity, according to his foreknowledge of all things." Here it is speaking of the order of the High Priests before Christ: their order being after the order of the Son of God, and this order being without beginning of days or end of years, being prepared from eternity to all eternity. This being Christ's order, He being from eternity to all eternity, has held this holy order of priesthood from eternity and will hold it to all eternity. Those High Priests before Christ came into the world, held this holy order of priesthood as a type of Christ's order; but when Christ came into the world, he then claimed his own holy order of priesthood and power on earth, doing away with all types and shadows under the old law, himself alone being our great and last High Priest unto whom we can go to obtain mercy and find grace to help in time of need. Brethren, I am constrained to say as Alma says at his conclusion of this matter: He ends his writing in the tenth chapter, 2d paragraph, by these words: "Now I need not rehearse the matter; what I have said, may suffice. Behold, the scriptures are before you; if ye will wrest them it shall be to your own destruction."

CHAPTER X

THE CHOICE SEER.

As ancient Israel was in error in misinterpreting prophecy, so the Latter Day Saints are in error in misinterpreting modern prophecy. As I have said, a distinction must be made between the gospel or doctrine of Christ, and prophecy. It is plain to be seen from the scriptures that it is not the Lord's purpose to reveal prophecy in as great plainness as the gospel and doctrine of Christ. Scripture prophecy refers to events that are to transpire in the Lord's work; and it is not his purpose to reveal in plainness at this time, all the mysteries and plans of his great work among the children of men in the future. Such has been the case in all ages past. The prophecies to the Jews regarding the way in which Christ was to come, were obscure, and they were only understood by those who had the spirit to understand them. They could have been written so plain that any person could understand them correctly; but it was not God's purpose to do so. The Book of Mormon tells us that the book of prophecy of John's Revelation is hard to understand, but when God's own due time comes, it is to be unfolded and made plain; but the gospel and doctrine of Christ is so plain in the New Covenant of the Book of Mormon, that a child can understand it. Christ says, "And I give you these commandments, because of the disputations which have been among you. And blessed are ye if ye have no disputations among you." Also, that you might "know of the true points of my (Christ's) doctrine." (Nephi viii:9 and ix:11). But prophecy is another matter outside of the gospel or doctrine of Christ; it can only be interpreted correctly by the enlightenment of the Holy Ghost. Peter says, "We have also a more sure word of 'prophecy'; whereunto ye do well that ye take heed, as unto a light that shineth in a dark place, until the day dawn, and the 'day star' arise in your hearts." (2 Peter i:19). The day star means the Holy Ghost, by which prophecy can only be rightly understood.

The Latter Day Saints are in error in believing that Joseph Smith was the Choice Seer spoken of in 2 Nephi ii.

I will show you that Brother Joseph could not have been this Choice Seer, because that Seer is to be of the seed of Joseph, (of Egypt) of the seed of Lehi, who is a descendant of Joseph, which Lehi came over to this land from Jerusalem 600 years B.C.: The American Indians (the

Lamanites) being the remnant of that seed. To make it more plain, I will repeat the explanation given in Chapter iii. The man who is not learned (in 2 Nephi xi:18) refers to Brother Joseph; But the Choice Seer (2 Nephi ii) is another man. He is to come from the fruit of the loins of Joseph (of Egypt), that seed being the branch which was broken off at Jerusalem, to whom this land was consecrated for their inheritance forever—being Lehi and his seed; Lehi's seed being Little Joseph, who received this blessing from his father Lehi, that his seed should not utterly be destroyed; for out of his seed which should not all be destroyed (the Indians), should come this Choice Seer. It is very plain to me. This Seer is to come from the Lamanites, and Brother Joseph is not of that seed. The name of that Seer will be Joseph, after Joseph of Egypt, and his father's name Joseph. He is to translate sealed records yet to come forth. "And not to the bringing forth my word only, saith the Lord, but to the *convincing* them of my word." Brother Joseph never convinced a single Lamanite that I ever heard of.

This Choice Seer is to convince the Lamanites in person, and do a great work among them ("his brethren") in person. It can plainly be seen by reading the two passages referred to, that "the man that is not learned" is a different man from this Choice Seer. There is no identity between the two persons referred to in these two passages. In one passage it calls the person referred to "the man that is not learned;" while in the other; the person referred to is a Choice Seer, who shall be great and mighty like unto Moses; and the whole chapter is devoted to this Seer and to Moses. Some have confounded the men spoken of in 2 Nephi xi:17, 18, 19. A man, being the spirit of a just man made perfect, had a hand in bringing forth the words of the Book of Mormon as well as Brother Joseph; and there is also a time referred to in the nineteenth paragraph that is yet in the future. We will now analyze this chapter (2 Nephi ii) concerning the Choice Seer. It is plain to be seen that the whole chapter refers to this one Choice Seer and to Moses. I see some of the Latter Day Saints have lately interpreted *"one mighty"* to arise from the Lamanites; this is a recent interpretation they have put upon this chapter. A clause in the last part of the chapter makes it very plain that the Choice Seer spoken of all through the chapter, is to come from the Lamanites. It is very plain that the last part of the chapter (Par. 4) refers to this same Choice Seer. Lehi is making his conclusion and closing remarks concerning his son's (little Joseph's) blessing; which blessing can be seen in the first part of the chapter, the blessing being this; that little Joseph's seed should not all be destroyed, for out of his seed should arise one mighty, who should be a Choice Seer.

"And now, behold, my son Joseph, after this manner did my father of old (Joseph of Egypt) prophesy. Wherefore, because of this covenant thou are blessed (a blessing); for thy seed shall not be destroyed * * * And there shall raise up *one mighty* among them (this same Choice Seer—this same blessing), who shall do much good, both in word and in deed, being an instrument in the hands of God, with exceeding faith, to work mighty wonders, and do that thing which is *great in the sight of God.*" Before this it says he shall be great in mine eyes. Why is it that any one cannot see this? The closing of this chapter is only a rehearsal and conclusion about this same Choice Seer.

This whole chapter treats of the one matter; a blessing is pronounced upon little Joseph, because a Great Seer is to be of his seed, that should not all be destroyed. That seed being "a branch which was to be broken off" at Jerusalem, to whom this land was consecrated for their inheritance. He tells them that this Great Seer was not the Messiah, but that he was to come from a branch of the house of Israel that was to be broken off, "nevertheless to be remembered in the covenants of the Lord, that the Messiah should be made manifest unto them in the latter days, in the spirit of power, unto the bringing of them out of darkness unto light; yea, out of hidden darkness and out of captivity unto freedom." Can you not see from this that the Choice Seer is to come from the Lamanites? They are the people here referred to. The next words are as follows: "For Joseph (of Egypt) truly testified, saying, a Seer shall the Lord my God raise up, who shall be a Choice Seer unto the fruit of my loins." This is the testimony or prophecy of Joseph (of Egypt) which Lehi refers to in his closing remarks in paragraph four, where he says: "And now, behold, my son Joseph, after this manner did my father of old prophesy. Wherefore because of this covenant thou art blessed; for thy seed shall not be destroyed, for they shall hearken unto the words of the book; and there shall raise up one mighty among them." They shall hearken unto the words of the book which the Choice Seer shall bring forth, which Seer is to convince them. This passage means the same as if the word *for* instead of the word *and* was there, as follows: "Wherefore, because of this covenant thou art blessed; for thy seed shall not be destroyed, for they shall hearken unto the words of the book; 'for' there shall raise up one mighty among them, who shall do much good, * * * and do that thing which is great in the sight of God."

Again, it says this Choice Seer will do only according to the commands of God. He will be faithful and break none of God's commandments. This alone proves that Brother Joseph was not the Choice Seer. In a revelation given to Brother Joseph while he was translating, (Sec. 2) the Lord said, "Behold, how oft have you transgressed the commandments and the laws of God, and have gone on in the persuasions of men * * * if thou art not aware thou wilt fall." Does this agree with the description of the Choice Seer? Nay verily. This alone should satisfy any one, and will satisfy any one who is not trusting in an arm of flesh, that Brother Joseph was not the Choice Seer.

Again, it can be seen from this point that Brother Joseph was not this Great Seer. He is to come from the seed that shall write the word of the Lord; and this is the Nephite seed. It says, "But a Seer will I raise up out of the fruit of thy loins; * * * wherefore, the fruit of thy loins (from which this Seer is to be raised up) shall *write;* (the Nephite records), and the fruit of the loins of Judah shall write." So we see again that the Choice Seer is to come from the Nephite or Lamanite seed.

Again, the same can be seen from a clause which follows in this connection: "and bringing them to the knowledge of their fathers in the latter days."

Again, the same can be seen from this clause which says, "He shall do a work for the fruit of thy loins, HIS BRETHREN, which shall be of great worth unto them, even to the bringing of them to the knowledge of the covenants which I have made with thy fathers." From this we see that his brethren are to be the Lamanites. Then he is to be of the Lamanite seed.

Again, it says, they who seek to destroy this Choice Seer shall be confounded. Those who sought to destroy Brother Joseph were not confounded, but they destroyed him.

Brethren, you have no conception of how great and mighty this Seer will be, and the great work he is to do in restoring the house of Israel, or you would never claim that Brother Joseph was this man. I believe this man to be the same man referred to in Genesis xlix:24, and by Paul in

Romans xi:26. The passage in Genesis is Joseph's blessing: "From thence is the Shepherd, the stone of Israel." From the seed of Joseph will come a man who shall be the Shepherd to gather scattered Israel in the last days. This does not mean Christ, for he came from the seed of Judah. The other passage in Romans says, "There shall come out of Sion (this land) the Deliverer, and shall turn away ungodliness from Jacob." This does not mean Christ, as you can see by reading the context. I am satisfied these two passages refer to this same Choice Seer.

To conclude, we see that Brother Joseph was not this Choice Seer for the following reasons:

First: He is to come from the seed of Lehi, and Joseph Smith is not of that seed.

Second: He is to convince the Lamanites in person; Joseph Smith did not convince them.

Third: His tongue will not be loosed that he can speak much, and the Lord is to raise up a spokesman for him; Joseph Smith's tongue was loosed to speak, he being a good speaker.

Fourth: Those who seek to destroy this Seer will be confounded, this does not agree as being Brother Joseph, because he was destroyed.

Fifth: The Choice Seer will be faithful and do strictly according to the command of God; Brother Joseph broke the commands of God from the beginning.

So we see that Brother Joseph was not this Choice Seer.

CHAPTER XI

THE GATHERING.

One of the greatest mistakes that the leaders of the old church made, and a mistake which the Latter Day Saints are making to-day, is concerning this matter.

The time for building the city New Jerusalem has not yet come. The leaders of the old church, in their unwise zeal, prompted more by the spirit of man than the Spirit of God to do great things in the Lord's vineyard, began to think that they were the few chosen servants who should labor in the last pruning of the vineyard, and do the great closing work of the last dispensation of the fullness of times—building the city New Jerusalem, etc. If they had been more humble and lowly in heart, they would not have made this great mistake. They did not stop to consider that God had his own time in which his great and marvelous works should be done among the inhabitants of the earth. They thought that the time for building the city New Jerusalem must be now at hand—in their time—man's time—and that they were the ones who were to build it. In this condition of heart, brought about by their unwise zeal and the spirit of man to do great things, instead of being humble, they had Brother Joseph to get a revelation as to the time of building that city, and gathering into it. So Brother Joseph gave a revelation, as mouthpiece, that the time was then at hand, and they began to gather into Jackson County, Missouri, at once. They were too hasty. The time to build that city had not yet come, because Christ says that the *"remnant of Jacob"* (the seed of Lehi, unto whom this land was consecrated) are the people who shall build that city, and the Gentiles are only to assist them to build it. The other people who shall also assist them to build that city are *"as many of the house of Israel as shall come"* into the covenant. Therefore if the seed of Lehi are to build that city, the leaders of the old church and the Latter Day Saints to-day are in error in this matter. I will show you from the Book of Mormon that the seed of Lehi, on whom the choicest blessing of any of the house of Israel rests, are the people who shall be honored with building that city; and that the rest of the house of Israel who are faithful, and also the Gentiles, shall only assist them in that work (Nephi x:1). Christ himself says: "And they (the Gentiles) shall assist my people, the remnant of Jacob; and also, as many of the house of Israel as shall come, that they may build a city, which shall be called the New Jerusalem; and then shall they assist my people that they (all) may be gathered in, who are scattered upon all the face of the land, in unto the New Jerusalem." From this we see the remnant of Jacob are the ones who shall build that city, and the Gentiles and the rest of the house of Israel shall only assist them. Now, the question is, what people does the *"remnant of Jacob"* here refer to? We find that Christ makes it plain in this same sermon he is preaching to them, that the *remnant of Jacob* means the remnant of the seed of Lehi. In the preceding chapter, paragraph eleven, Christ says as follows: "When these things * * * * shall be made known unto the Gentiles, that they may know concerning this people, who are a 'remnant of the house of Jacob,' and concerning this my people who shall be scattered by them." So we see that the *remnant of Jacob* means the Lamanites, or seed of Lehi. Then it is plain that the time to build that city has not yet come, because the *remnant of Jacob* is to do that work.

There is an expression that Christ uses in this chapter which is often used by the prophets; that expression is *"At that day."* All who understand the scriptures know that this expression means *in that dispensation of time*. A dispensation may be a thousand years, more or less; and the prophets all speak of a dispensation by saying *"at that day."* A day with the Lord is as a thousand years. Isaiah, when prophesying of events to take place in the same dispensation, but more than a thousand years apart, speaks of them in the same chapter by saying *"at that day"*; when a person who does not understand the scriptures might think from his language that the events were to transpire within a few years of each other. Some of the brethren have tried to prove that Brother Joseph was the Choice Seer because the text says of this man that he shall *"be made strong in that day* when my work shall *commence* among all my people," etc. *In that day* or *at that day* means in that dispensation or cycle of time; and it would be folly for us to attempt to locate the time of an event because it says *in that day*. The above text means as follows: In the dispensation of time in which the work of the Father shall commence to restore Israel, in that dispensation—in that day—the Choice Seer is to be made strong.

So also in this chapter concerning the building of the city New Jerusalem, in speaking of the time when the house of Israel shall be gathered in unto that city from all over the earth, a time when the power of heaven shall come down among them, a time when Jesus Christ will be in their midst, it says *at that day* shall the work of the Father *commence*, etc. Of course we understand the words *at that day* to mean in that dispensation of time, which may extend over a thousand years.

We suppose of course that the sealed records which are to come forth will give full instructions concerning the gathering in unto the city New Jerusalem, and the restoration of Israel that is now scattered among every nation under heaven. These great events are simply mentioned in the Book of Mormon and the Bible. I believe that no man living in the flesh has ever had any conception of the great and marvelous work of the Lord which is yet to transpire in gathering the house of Israel. The coming forth of the Book of Mormon is only a preparatory work. It is only an abridgement of the sealed records of the Nephites. Records are yet to come forth which "reveal all things from the foundation of the world unto the end thereof"; all things which have been done, and all things which are yet to be done—the great and wondrous mysteries and the works of God which are yet to transpire.

CHAPTER XII

CHANGING THE NAME OF THE CHURCH.

When Christ established His church upon this land, in the days of the Nephites, He gave them special instructions from his own lips concerning the name by which His church must be called. He gave them a strict commandment to call the church by His name, which He said was *Christ*. The Nephite brethren obeyed that commandment and called the church "THE CHURCH OF CHRIST," as seen in many places in the New Covenant of the Book of Mormon. And after this time, in no place in the book is it called by any other name. Christ himself considered this matter of the name of His church of great importance, as can be seen from His instructions regarding it. The Nephite brethren were having disputations among themselves as to the name of the church, just as there are disputations at this day concerning this matter. When Christ appeared to them on the third day of His mission upon this land, the first thing they said to him was this (Nephi xii:3): "Lord, we will that Thou wouldst tell us the name whereby we shall call this church; for there are disputations among the people concerning this matter. And the Lord said unto them, Verily, verily I say unto you, why is it that the people should murmur and dispute because of this thing? Have they not read the scriptures, which say, ye must take upon you the NAME OF CHRIST, which is my name? for by this name shall ye be called at the last day; * * * * therefore, ye shall call *the church* in my name; * * * * and how be it my church, save it be called in my name? For if a church be called in Moses' name, then it be Moses' church; or if it be called in the name of a man, then it be the church of a man; but if it be called in my name, then it is my church, if it so be that they are built upon my gospel." So we see that Christ himself considered this matter of great importance. If he had wanted them to call it by the name *Jesus Christ* he would have said so, but he said the name *Christ*. Remember brethren, how the words of the Book of Mormon came; not by the wisdom of any man, but by the wisdom and power of God; therefore, every word is in its place. In June, 1829, the Lord gave us the name by which we must call the church, being the same as He gave the Nephites. We obeyed His commandment, and called it THE CHURCH OF CHRIST until 1834, when, through the influence of Sydney Rigdon, the name of the church was changed to "The Church of the Latter Day Saints," dropping out the name of Christ entirely, that name which we were strictly commanded to call the church by, and which

Christ by His own lips makes so plain. Now it is strange, it is marvelous, that the Latter Day Saints to-day consider this matter of changing the name of the church, and the leaders in 1834 dropping out the name of Christ, as a small thing and a light matter! You know not how strict are the commands of God! It is nothing short of trifling with a strict commandment of Almighty God, and setting at naught the decision of Christ himself when He decided this matter so plainly and so positively, when there were disputations regarding it. I say, that any man who sanctions the name of the church being changed from the name which Christ gave it, setting aside the decision of Christ in this matter, is in utter spiritual blindness, and should repent speedily. Suppose that the Nephite brethren, five years after Christ had ascended into heaven, had said among themselves: "Brethren, although Christ commanded us to call the church THE CHURCH OF CHRIST, let us change the name which He gave the church, and drop out the name of Christ, which He commanded the church to be called by, and call this church the Church of Former Day Saints." Can you not see they would have been under condemnation for it? Answer this question yourselves. This is what the leaders did in 1834, when they changed the name to the "Church of the Latter Day Saints," dropping out the name of Christ. Still you claim they were not in spiritual blindness. Verily, you know not God's way of dealing with man. His commandments are strict. Remember Uzzah, who broke a command of God by reaching out his hand to steady the ark, thinking that he was doing God's will; but was stricken dead for it.

I will give you what is on the title page of the Book of Commandments, and also the Book of Doctrine and Covenants, concerning the name, to show you that the name of the church was changed, and the name of Christ dropped out entirely. On the title page of the Book of Commandments is this: "A BOOK OF COMMANDMENTS FOR THE GOVERNMENT OF THE CHURCH OF CHRIST." On the title page of the Book of Doctrine and Covenants, published at Kirtland, Ohio, 1835, is this: "DOCTRINE AND COVENANTS OF THE CHURCH OF THE LATTER DAY SAINTS." Also, the heading of the preface reads thus: "TO THE MEMBERS OF THE CHURCH OF THE LATTER DAY SAINTS." Also on page 5: "THEOLOGY. LECTURE FIRST. ON THE DOCTRINE OF THE CHURCH OF THE LATTER DAY SAINTS." You see they changed the name of the church, and left out the name of

Christ entirely, which the church was strictly commanded to wear, or else they were not the Church of Christ.

Some of you have referred to Nephi, son of Nephi, i:8, where it says those who believed in Christ were called Nephites, Jacobites, Josephites and Zoramites; but if you will read that passage you will see that it was the wicked Lamanites who called the believers by these names. This was 231 years after Christ, when divisions had taken place in the church. The church at Jerusalem after Christ, and the church upon this land before Christ came, was often alluded to *by men* speaking of it, by various names, as the Church of the Lamb of God; the Church of God, etc: as some writers today would allude to it by various names; speaking of it as the Church of the Saints of God, etc., but that is not the question. The question is, what name was the church to wear—what name did Christ want His church to take upon themselves? What name did Christ command them to take? It is important for every public institution to have a name. It is important for any church organization to have a name. Christ considered it of great importance for His church to have a name, and he gave it a name, telling them that it was necessary for His church to wear a certain name, and that if they wore any other name, that they were not His church. Are you so blinded that you cannot see and understand this? What right has any man or men to change the name which Christ decided the church should wear? God have mercy upon the man who says that the name should be changed to any other than that which Christ gave us. As for myself, I will take the decision of the King of Heaven in this matter; all those who are willing to trifle with the word of God, and set aside the decision of Christ, may do so. I speak as to wise men; judge ye what I say.

Brethren, I have this to say in conclusion. I will not argue and dispute with you. In the spirit of love and meekness I have told you in plain and simple words what the Spirit of God has moved upon me to speak. I am now past eighty-two years of age, and my work in this world is about done. God has given to this generation the Book of Mormon, and how plain and simple is the doctrine of Christ set forth therein. Now brethren, remember—remember the words of Him who reigns in heaven and on earth; which will ye hear, the words of our Lord Jesus Christ in that which is written, or the words of man? Choose for yourselves whom you will hear. I am not asking you to hear me; I refer you to the words of eternal truth, as they are contained in the two sacred books. I will always pray for you, that you may some day see that you are in error in believing and teaching the doctrines which men have added to the doctrine of Christ.

My days to stay here are not many more; I soon go to rest with those who have gone before me; but I have rid my garments of your blood and the blood of all men. You may not understand by what spirit I speak, until at the judgment bar of God; then you will understand. May God have mercy upon you to humble your hearts before him, that you may be guided into the light of truth, is my prayer through the name of Christ. Amen.

DAVID WHITMER Richmond, Mo., April 1st, 1887.

www.ingramcontent.com/pod-product-compliance
Lightning Source LLC
LaVergne TN
LVHW041633070426
835507LV00008B/591